The National Real Estate Salesperson License Exam Prep Book

2024-25 Edition

Pass & Excel, Master the Exam with In-Depth Insights and Comprehensive Strategies to Succeed Nationwide

Abbot Wardman

UNLOCK ESSENTIAL EXTRA STUDY TOOLS!

Before diving into the chapters,
SCAN THE QR CODE at the end of this book
to access a suite of extra free valuable resources — including:

> ➤ **AUDIO SCENARIOS**
>
> ➤ **FLASHCARDS**
>
> ➤ **STUDY GUIDES**
>
> ➤ **EXTRA TESTS**

These materials are designed to significantly enhance your learning experience. **Download them immediately** to ensure you don't miss out on these **crucial aids for your Real Estate Exam preparation**.

DON'T MISS OUT ON YOUR STUDY BOOSTERS!

Follow the social page of our international community for updates, news, and surprises!
Scan the QR code and join the facebook page

"The National Real Estate Salesperson License Exam Prep"

Table of Contents

Introduction

Welcome to the start of an exciting new career in real estate! As someone eager to transition into this dynamic industry, you have taken an important first step in seeking out this comprehensive exam prep guide. Passing the real estate salesperson licensing exam is the key that unlocks access to a world of opportunity. This book will ensure you're able to ace the test and leverage your people skills and passion for properties into a thriving career.

Real estate professionals facilitate one of life's biggest transactions—finding a home. Beyond just selling properties, you will assist families in navigating the exhilarating but often complex process of securing shelter. Your skills will provide comfort and security, all while unleashing your entrepreneurial talents. It is a job for keen negotiators and clever problem solvers who can balance razor-sharp business instincts with genuine compassion for clients' needs.

While a flair for sales and charisma are invaluable real estate assets, simply being a "people person" is not enough. Success requires comprehensive knowledge spanning property laws, market analysis, contracts, financing procedures, and much more. Only with full command of the industry's regulations and intricacies can you thrive in this competitive field.

That is where this guide comes in. Consider it your handbook for launching a prosperous real estate career, packed with the precise information you need to pass the exam and apply skills daily as a licensed salesperson. With focused study, the licensing test need not be intimidating—view it instead as your first stepping stone into an industry ripe with potential.

This book methodically breaks down the multi-layered real estate industry, tackling both broad foundations as well as state-specific nuances. Consider this your personal roadmap for exam success. I will elucidate what to expect on test day, prime you with study strategies, and provide numerous opportunities to practice and assess your grasp of the material. With the knowledge garnered from these pages, you will walk into the exam room with confidence.

I will begin by exploring theoretical foundations—the principles that underpin real estate transactions. What exactly constitutes ownership of a property? How do governmental bodies and environmental regulations impact land usage? How are properties valued and financed? You will learn the answers to these questions and more in the first half of the book. I will demystify real estate law and contracts, agency relationships, and the step-by-step process of buying and selling properties. Whether you are a complete novice or have some prior experience, these chapters will cement your understanding of real estate's core concepts.

Since the industry varies significantly across states, I will also spotlight guidelines specific to the 10 states where real estate is most active. You will learn about state licensing procedures, real estate commissions, and contractual rules unique to these areas. I realize you may be seeking a license in a different state, but this cross-section will give you a valuable window into how localized laws govern the industry.

In the second half of the book, I will switch gears to practical exam prep. I will provide study tips, share time management strategies, and supply numerous sample scenarios and quizzes. These exercises allow you to test your knowledge, pinpoint deficiencies, and assess readiness for the real exam experience. I will also include a math workbook tailored to real estate calculations. You will gain confidence performing crucial computations like commissions, mortgage interest, property taxes, and more.

By the time you reach the final mock exam, you will have a comprehensive review of all test material under your belt. Our sample national and state sections with answer explanations will indicate where you stand. Use it as a barometer of comprehension and a predictor of how you will fare on the actual licensing test. If any sections prove challenging, I encourage you to revisit the corresponding chapters and quizzes for reinforcement until the material is second nature.

With focused study, I am confident this guide equips you with everything required to begin an exciting career in the dynamic world of real estate. Let's get started!

Section I: Theoretical Knowledge
Chapter 1: Property Ownership and Land Use

Property ownership and land use form the foundation of real estate transactions and practices. To become a successful real estate agent, one must have a deep understanding of the types of property ownership, land characteristics, government rights, and environmental laws related to real estate. This chapter will provide an in-depth look at these crucial topics.

Types of Ownership

The ownership of real property comes in many forms, each with its own unique rights and limitations. Knowing the nuances of different ownership types, allows real estate professionals to better serve their clients' interests during property transfers and utilization. Besides sole ownership, the main types of ownership are joint tenancy, tenancy in common, and community property.

Sole Ownership

Sole ownership refers to a property being owned exclusively by one person or entity. The sole owner has complete control over the property and can sell, lease, or transfer it at their discretion. Sole ownership provides full autonomy in decision-making regarding the property without needing approval from others. However, the sole owner also bears all liabilities associated with the property. If the property accrues debt or is sued, the sole owner is fully responsible. Sole ownership works well for single individuals purchasing property for themselves. It also allows entities like corporations to maintain clear ownership.

Joint Tenancy

Joint tenancy describes a form of concurrent ownership where two or more people own a property and hold the same rights over it. The key defining feature is the Right of Survivorship. If one of the owners dies, their share transfers to the surviving owners automatically. This avoids lengthy probate procedures. To create a joint tenancy, the owners must share four unities: time, title, interest, and possession. All owners must receive their interest through the same deed transaction and document. They must hold equal shares and equivalent possession rights. Joint tenancy works well for spouses, partners, and joint purchases between trusted parties. However, joint tenancy does limit each owner's autonomy over the property.

Tenancy in Common

Under tenancy in common, at least two people hold ownership interests in a specific property. As with joint tenancy, this creates concurrent ownership. However, each owner holds a separate, distinct share of the property. One owner can sell their share or transfer it in a will without consent from the other owners. One big difference is that there is no Right of Survivorship. If one of the owners dies, their interest goes to that person's heirs, not the remaining owners. Owners can hold unequal shares, like a 70/30 split. Tenancy in common is favorable when owners want more flexibility in transferring property or wish to hold unequal shares based on contribution amount. It removes the restraints of joint tenancy. However, it may create complicated transfers if multiple heirs inherit shares.

Community Property

In some states, the law says that property that is acquired during a marriage is considered property owned jointly as well as equally by both spouses and it is called community property. The exact ownership share depends on state law, with some mandating completely equal 50/50 splits. Under community property, both spouses must agree to sell, lease, or mortgage the property even though one spouse may be listed as the sole titleholder. If the couple divorces, the community property is divided equitably between spouses. Community property principles only apply in select states. Real estate agents must be aware of a state's community property laws when working with married clients.

Land Characteristics and Descriptions

To utilize land profitably and legally, real estate professionals must understand the characteristics and descriptions of real property. Factors like zoning codes, parcel boundaries, soil composition, and mineral rights all influence how land can be developed, transferred, or restricted. Land appraisals also rely heavily on classifications and qualitative descriptions. By learning proper terminology and land description methods, real estate professionals can accurately convey property details during transactions.

Physical Characteristics

Physical characteristics include the tangible, natural features of land. Common characteristics include topography, hydrology, vegetation, soil, and geological formations. Factors like elevation, grade, water access, and soil quality can impact property values and permitted land uses. When listing land, real estate agents should include details on salient physical features per surveying data and assessment reports. They should also alert buyers to any natural hazards like flooding zones, wildfire risks, or seismic faults affecting the land.

Parcel Boundaries and Zoning

Understanding parcel boundaries and zoning classifications is crucial when transferring property rights. Boundary lines demarcate the extent of a land parcel using methods like metes and bounds and township/range descriptions. Proper boundary recording prevents disputes with neighboring landowners. Zoning codes limit allowable development and activities on a parcel, specifying if residential, commercial, or industrial uses are permitted. Real estate professionals must verify zoning to ensure the buyer's intended usage aligns with local regulations before purchase. This prevents issues like prohibited commercial buildings on residential lots.

Mineral and Water Rights

Subsurface elements like groundwater, oil, gas, and mineral deposits belong to whoever holds the mineral or water rights for the land. By default, these rights transfer to surface landowners in many areas. However, previous owners may have severed these rights and sold them to other parties via mineral deeds or leases. Real estate agents must verify who holds the mineral rights in question and if any encumbrances like oil and gas leases exist on the property. Discrepancies between surface ownership and mineral/water rights can cause major issues down the line.

Easements and Restrictions

Easements and deed restrictions also limit property rights. Easements allow third parties like utility companies to access portions of the land for managing infrastructure like pipelines or transmission lines. Deed restrictions prohibit certain uses for the property, like commercial activity in a residential subdivision. Real estate professionals must disclose any easements or restrictions to buyers, as they can severely limit development potential down the road if unknown. A proper title review will uncover these encumbrances.

Government Rights in Land

While property owners hold certain rights, government powers can substantially regulate private land usage and transfer. Through taxation, eminent domain, zoning, and escheat, governmental entities can extract value from properties or restrict certain activities. Real estate professionals require a working knowledge of these government rights to advise clients when buying, selling, or developing land. This overview will provide that requisite knowledge.

Property Taxation

Local governments impose annual property taxes on privately owned land and buildings within their jurisdiction. While unpopular with some landowners, property taxes provide essential municipal revenue. Property assessors valuate parcels, and this assessed value determines the annual tax amount. Appraisal factors include property type, age, location, and use. Property taxes stay with the property when it sells, transferring to new owners. Real estate agents must educate buyers on carrying costs like property taxes to avoid post-purchase surprises. Agents also need expertise on property tax exemptions, like those for senior citizens.

Eminent Domain

Under eminent domain power, federal and state governments can force the sale of private property for public benefit, even without the owner's consent. Common uses include infrastructure like highways, public parks, and utility corridors. Land seized via eminent domain must be for legitimate public use and requires just compensation for owners. Compensation may be below market value, though. Real estate professionals must alert clients that needed lands for public projects face eminent domain potential. Eminent domain represents a limitation on private property powers.

Zoning and Land Use Restrictions

Municipal zoning and land use regulations significantly impact real estate practices. Zoning controls property uses in specific geographic zones, dictating allowable structures, heights, density, setbacks, and permitted activities. Land use regulations may restrict development in sensitive areas like wetlands and shorelines or prohibit certain businesses in neighborhoods. These governmental powers limit owners' full utilization of their real estate. Real estate professionals must be experts in local zoning and land use rules to avoid the frustrations of prohibited projects. Knowing these parameters allows agents to match buyers to compliant properties.

Property Escheat

When individuals die with no heirs, their property may escheat to the state, meaning their land transfers to government ownership. States can then liquidate the assets. Escheat can also occur if owners fail to pay taxes or neglect vacant properties. Professionals must understand escheat laws to fully inform clients about heirs, wills, and tax delinquency. With escheat, governmental bodies, not relatives, become default property owners - a rare limitation on private land ownership.

Environmental Laws and Real Estate

Federal and state environmental regulations significantly impact many real estate deals, thus requiring agent expertise on these nuanced laws. From site contamination to wetlands protection, environmental considerations overlay property use and development. Understanding key statutes and agency rules allows real estate professionals to facilitate smooth transactions while ensuring regulatory compliance. This section provides a robust overview of major environmental laws affecting real estate practice.

Hazardous Waste and Superfund Sites

Hazardous waste regulations heavily influence land usage. The Resource Conservation and Recovery Act (RCRA) regulates hazardous waste as well as non-hazardous waste handling from generation to disposal. Comprehensive Environmental Response, Compensation and Liability Act (CERCLA) mandates the cleanup of contamination at Superfund sites with strict liability standards. Real estate agents must identify properties with past commercial/industrial uses at risk of containing contaminants. Full environmental assessments are critical before purchasing a property to avoid massive cleanup liability. RCRA and CERCLA site risks carry huge due diligence responsibilities.

Wetlands Protection

Complex regulations protect wetlands environments from development impacts. Section 404 of the Clean Water Act prohibits draining or filling wetlands without U.S. Army Corps permits, which face high burdens. Wetlands are also covered under state laws and county stormwater rules. Real estate professionals must identify potential wetlands using surveys and prudent site inspection. Caution is needed as small, unmapped wetlands still fall under regulatory jurisdiction. Agents must disclose the presence of wetlands and permit needs to prevent unallowed property alterations post-purchase.

Endangered Species Habitat

The Endangered Species Act includes strong protections for the habitats of listed species. Actions that harm protected habitats can face severe penalties. Real estate agents must research if protected species reside on or near the property through U.S. Fish and Wildlife Service consultations. Endangered habitats bring development limitations and sometimes bar any land alterations. Real estate professionals have an ESA duty to properly disclose protected site uses to interested buyers before transactions. Lack of habitat knowledge causes headaches later.

Permitting and Impact Assessments

Construction permitting often requires costly environmental impact assessments. Developments with substantial land alterations must receive State Environmental Policy Act (SEPA) permits, requiring assessments of factors like runoff, wildlife, vegetation, traffic, and historical artifacts. Local shoreline permits mandate additional reviews for properties near bodies of water. Real estate professionals must factor in long lead times and the costs of assessments and permitting to value land accurately. Comparing zoning restrictions and past impact studies offers worthwhile insights for buyers before purchase agreements.

Chapter 2: Real Estate Law

Real estate transactions occur within a complex framework of laws and regulations at the federal, state, and local levels. To successfully facilitate deals, agents must understand core legal principles governing property transfers, ownership rights, title conveyance, contracts, liens, easements, and disclosures. This chapter provides an in-depth exploration of pivotal real estate law domains. It covers key federal statutes and regulatory bodies while also delving into crucial state-level laws. You will gain legal knowledge essential for compliant, informed practice and develop a keen awareness of issues to safeguard clients against. With a firm grasp of real estate's legal landscape, professionals can seamlessly guide transactions and uphold high ethical standards.

Federal Real Estate Laws

Although states hold primary real estate authority, federal legislation also substantially impacts the industry. From fair housing to financing regulations, familiarity with federal real estate law empowers professionals to keep deals compliant across jurisdictions. This section surveys major statutes, regulatory bodies, tax policies, and programs at the federal level. The knowledge forms an indispensable legal baseline for success.

Fair Housing Act

The Fair Housing Act (FHA) enshrines anti-discrimination protections for home sales and rentals. Sellers and landlords cannot refuse housing based on religion, sex, race, color, national origin, familial status, or disability. FHA violations spur civil lawsuits and fines. Real estate agents also face punishment for discriminatory actions, such as racial steering. Strict adherence to fair housing principles is a legal and ethical mandate. Savvy professionals recognize the business case for broad inclusion.

Truth in Lending Act

The Truth in Lending Act (TILA) promotes transparency in lending. It requires clear disclosure of all costs and terms for real estate loans and mortgages. This allows borrowers to accurately compare options. Under TILA, lenders must provide a truth in the lending statement and a good faith estimate of all costs. Real estate professionals often counsel clients on loans, so TILA knowledge ensures proper guidance in evaluating lending offers. TILA facilitates informed comparison shopping.

Anti-Money Laundering Laws

Rigorous anti-money laundering (AML) laws apply to real estate deals. The Bank Secrecy Act requires that cash payments over $10,000 be reported. Additional FinCEN and PATRIOT Act rules mandate vetting clients for money laundering links and reporting suspicious activities. Given their client oversight duties, real estate professionals must be vigilant for red flags like unusual funding sources. Strict adherence to AML laws is vital to avoid harsh criminal penalties. Savvy agents proactively incorporate AML best practices.

RESPA and Consumer Protection

The Real Estate Settlement Procedures Act (RESPA) regulates residential closings. It prohibits kickbacks while allowing reasonable compensation. RESPA also mandates disclosures, including a good faith estimate, mortgage servicing notice, and more. The Consumer Financial Protection Bureau (CFPB) oversees RESPA compliance and broader consumer protection laws for real estate transactions. Knowledge of required RESPA procedures and CFPB oversight empowers professionals to steer clear of violations.

Federal Tax Deductions

Tax policies incentivize homeownership. Mortgage interest as well as property taxes can are deductible on federal returns. Gains from home sales may qualify for capital gains exclusion after two years of primary residency. First-time homebuyer tax credits have also been offered. Real estate professionals should be well-versed in current federal tax deductions and credits related to real estate. This allows proper counseling of clients on the tax implications of homeownership.

HUD and FHA Loans

Federal agencies significantly impact real estate financing. The Department of Housing and Urban Development (HUD) oversees housing programs and fair practices. The Federal Housing Administration (FHA) insures qualified mortgages, opening homeownership to more buyers as a consequence. FHA loans require lower down payments but charge mortgage insurance premiums. Real estate professionals should understand qualification criteria to match buyers with FHA products. HUD and FHA efforts expand and facilitate financing.

State-Specific Real Estate Laws

While federal laws establish baseline real estate rules, states hold primary authority over property rights and transactions. State statutes and regulations vary widely on key issues like commissions, disclosures, licensing, and more. Therefore, real estate professionals must be experts on their state's specific laws governing agency representation, required paperwork, and prohibited practices. This section provides an instructive national survey of major state real estate law differences.

Agency Relationships

States take different approaches to agency relationships between agents, buyers, and sellers. Some use statutory broker agency models defining set duties. Others allow for more fluid common law relationships with looser obligations. Agents must understand their state's agency principles, whether mandated disclosures are needed, and what fiduciary responsibilities exist. Agency law gets complex with dual agency. Vetting state rules helps avoid undisclosed conflicts of interest.

Disclosure Requirements

Property disclosures protect buyers from latent defects and material facts. States have varying requirements on issues that must be disclosed, like mold, deaths, structural conditions, and more. Timelines for reporting lead paint hazards also differ. Real estate professionals must track required disclosures, integrating robust checklists into transactions. Meticulous disclosure adherence demonstrates a duty of care and averts legal jeopardy.

Commissions and Compensation

Commission structures are not federally regulated, so states implement widely varying policies. Some cap percentages, while others prohibit certain commission-sharing arrangements as anti-competitive. Professional associations may provide guidance. State-specific commission customs should guide listing prices. Moreover, agent compensation disclosures often must be acknowledged by parties. Understanding state commission norms and rules is imperative.

Licensing Requirements

All states require real estate licenses, but prerequisites and procedures vary. Some mandate training before licensing exams, while others allow simultaneous education. Continuing education requirements also differ across states. Professionals must know their state's specific qualifications to maintain an active, compliant license. Reciprocal licensing allows practice in multiple states, but familiarity with each state's requirements is crucial.

Home Inspection Parameters

Home inspection requirements and inspectors' legal liability differ among states. In some, inspectors merely note issues. In others, they guarantee findings or determine a property's habitability. Some states mandate certain inspection report components. Real estate professionals should be well-versed in local home inspection customs and standards to best counsel buyers and transaction parties.

Specialized State Laws

Various unique real estate laws exist in specific states. For example, Maryland uses ground rent leases, while Georgia and Virginia use property surveys. Hawaii has compulsory seller disclosures. Washington mandates certain timber contract provisions. Professionals should identify any noteworthy specialized laws in their state and ensure full compliance.

Ownership and Title Transfer

Conveying clear property title is central to real estate deals. Professionals must grasp ownership rights, title transfer processes, joint tenancy and community property nuances, and liens' impact on the title. This knowledge allows for the proper drafting of sales contracts, deeds, and disclosures to efficiently shift ownership interests between parties after validating title clarity. Handling ownership issues carefully prevents future challenges.

Rights of Ownership

Ownership rights include the use, exclusion, disposition, and enjoyment of property. However, owners also have duties, such as taxes, maintenance, and avoiding harm to others through their property. Owners can relinquish rights via easements and restrictions. Real estate professionals must communicate ownership rights and obligations to clients to establish expectations and properly value properties. Knowing the boundaries of ownership prevents issues.

Title Search and Insurance

Title companies research property title records to verify legal ownership and uncover any encumbrances. This title search protects buyers via title insurance policies covering losses from undiscovered claims against the property. Real estate agents commonly coordinate title searches with buyers. Understanding the title process helps agents provide status updates and gives insight into researching title history independently.

Deeds to Transfer Ownership

Deeds formally transfer ownership of real estate. Different deed types have specific applications, legal language, and protections against future claims. Most deeds identify legal property descriptions, names of grantor and grantee, conveyance guarantees, and purchase price. Deeds must satisfy formal execution and delivery requirements to achieve legal validity. Real estate professionals must select the appropriate deed type for each transaction, such as warranty, quitclaim, and special purpose deeds.

Joint Tenancy and Community Property

Some forms of shared property ownership have special legal implications. Under joint tenancy, co-owners receive undivided interest of equal amount with the right of survivorship. Community property in select states conveys joint ownership and control between spouses. Agents must understand the rights and title transfer requirements for joint tenancy and community property to properly facilitate related sales. Married sellers may require additional documentation.

Title Issues and Dispute Resolution

At times, title flaws impede transactions, such as ownership gaps, missing heirs, liens, and unclear property descriptions. Real estate professionals should educate clients on options to resolve title disputes, including title insurance claims, quiet lawsuit actions, and deciding whether to proceed with an imperfect title conveyance through curative deeds. Competent agents can quickly address title problems and keep deals smoothly on track to closing.

Liens and Easements

Liens and easements represent two common encumbrances that can complicate real estate titles. Liens are third-party claims on the property, generally for unpaid debts. Easements entitle other parties to specific, limited property uses. Real estate professionals must be well-versed in lien payoffs, releases, and subordinations, as well as easement assignments and extinguishment. This allows proper processing of encumbered properties during sales.

Types of Liens

Many types of liens exist, with mortgage liens being most common in real estate. Other liens include mechanics' liens by contractors, homeowners' association liens for unpaid dues, legal judgment liens from lawsuits, and tax liens by the IRS and local government. Liens attach different foreclosure rights and repayment priorities. Professionals should know lien characteristics and be ready to counsel clients on resolving lien issues before closing.

Payoffs and Releases

For properties with liens, real estate professionals must coordinate proper lien payoffs with settlement funds and record lien releases following repayment. Without releases, titles stay clouded, that is to say with encumbrances. Agents often assist buyers in navigating the payoff process and provide release documentation for settlement. Understanding lien technicalities like partial releases avoids obstacles during the transaction.

Subordinations

At times, existing liens need subordination agreements where the lender agrees to subordinate their repayment priority under a new loan. This facilitates obtaining new mortgages needed for purchase. Real estate professionals should know when subordinations are advisable and the procedures for securing and recording these agreements pre-closing. Subordinations preserve existing liens while enabling necessary new financing.

Easement Assignments

Existing easements burdening a property can transfer to the new owner. However, buyers will often require an assignment document from the easement holder formally consenting to the transfer. Real estate professionals must know when easement assignments are prudent and how to request and obtain them to preempt any access disputes. Recorded assignments provide legal clarity.

Easement Extinguishment

When an easement no longer benefits the holder, real estate professionals can negotiate extinguishment agreements to remove the encumbrance from the title. This requires consent from the easement owner, which may require compensation. However, removal opens development potential, so extinguishment offers value. Agents are able to pursue strategic extinguishment, smooth transactions, and unlock property upside.

Chapter 3: Real Estate Finance

Financing represents the lifeblood of real estate transactions. Helping clients secure optimal funding aligned with their needs and goals is a key service real estate professionals provide. From prequalification to closing, agents guide buyers through the complex mortgage process. Sound financial knowledge equips professionals with the ability to offer sage loan counseling while ensuring transactions stay compliant and on track. This chapter provides a robust overview of real estate financing concepts, practices, and procedures. Topics span financing fundamentals, loan varieties, lender differences, government programs, qualifying applications, and creative finance solutions. This knowledge empowers new professionals to hit the ground running and distinguish themselves as informed financing authorities.

Real Estate Financing Basics

Smart real estate professionals build a strong foundation in financing fundamentals. This section covers core concepts like mortgage interest, calculations, terminology, risks, and prequalification essentials. Mastering the basics allows more nuanced guidance later when advising buyers on tailored financing decisions. Whether discussing deals with clients or providing industry insight to the public, mastery in core financing concepts proves indispensable.

Mortgage Interest

Interest makes up the cost of borrowing money for real estate loans. Lenders charge annual percentage interest on the loan balance. Monthly payments cover both the principal loan as well as interest. Fixed-rate mortgages have consistent interest for the full term. Adjustable-rate mortgages begin with lower teaser rates that later fluctuate based on market indexes. Knowing current interest norms and trajectories helps buyers make informed financing decisions.

Loan Calculations

Key calculations help determine affordable loan amounts for buyers. Monthly payments derive from multiplying the loan balance by the interest rate factor. Total costs include principal, interest, taxes, insurance, and any homeowner association dues. The front/back-end debt-to-income ratios benchmark qualifying capacity based on monthly expenses and income. Real estate professionals should be knowledgeable about these key computations.

Financing Terminology

Real estate financing utilizes many technical terms. Professionals must understand verbiages like points, PITI, amortization, discount points, origination fees, appraisal gaps, PMI, and APRs when advising clients and comparing loans. Fluency in financing terminology engenders trust and competent service. Clients will rely heavily on agents to decode mortgage language.

Loan Risks

While financing enables property purchases, loans do carry risks. Default may result in foreclosure. Rising interest rates on adjustable-rate mortgages increase payments. Balloon payments demand refinancing. Home values that drop below loan balance create negative equity. Agents should outline these risks so clients make informed financing choices appropriate for their risk tolerance and financial profile.

Prequalification vs. Preapproval

Prequalification utilizes estimated income and debts to gauge probable loan eligibility. Preapproval represents a lender's tentative commitment after full income verification. Preapproved buyers become highly qualified bidders, though final approval depends on the property appraisal. Professionals should prequalify clients early and coach them on the documentation needed for successful preapproval if they are serious home shoppers.

Types of Loans and Lenders

Today's real estate financing options are highly diverse. From conventional to unconventional loans in both the public and private sectors, many varieties exist. Professionals must understand key loan types available through different lending institutions to match clients effectively. This section details popular mortgage varieties and distinctions between lender categories to inform financing guidance.

Conventional Mortgages

Conventional mortgages are standard home loans not insured by any government agency. They offer competitive interest rates to borrowers with established credit and income. Conventional loans come in fixed and adjustable interest rate versions. Private lenders like banks and credit unions mainly issue conventional mortgages, which comprise most real estate loans today.

FHA Mortgages

FHA mortgages are government-insured loans requiring just a 3.5% down payment for qualifying borrowers. They expand financing access for first-time and moderate-income homebuyers. FHA mortgages do require mortgage insurance premiums. Large lenders and community banks often offer FHA products marketed directly to eligible borrowers.

VA and USDA Loans

Specific government mortgage programs assist military families and rural communities. VA loans help veterans and service members purchase property with no down payment. USDA loans support low-income buyers in rural areas. Real estate professionals should understand qualification criteria to connect appropriate buyers with these specialized loans.

Jumbo Mortgages

Jumbo mortgages are private larger loans exceeding conforming limits for conventional mortgages. Jumbos accommodate pricier properties in costlier markets. Requirements are stricter, and interest rates are higher than conforming loans. Wealth managers at major banks often handle jumbo products for high-net-worth individuals.

Alt-A and Non-Qualified Mortgages

Alt-A and non-qualified mortgages facilitate financing for borrowers unable to get prime mortgages. Standards are less stringent, but rates are higher. Independent lenders specializing in alternative products, not major banks, typically offer these loans. Real estate professionals can explain these as financing solutions for unique client situations.

Portfolio Lenders vs. Wholesale Lenders

Two primary mortgage lender categories exist. Portfolio lenders are local banks and credit unions financing loans from their own funds. Wholesale lenders are mortgage companies selling loans to investors. Portfolio lenders often offer greater flexibility for challenging applications and personalized service. However, wholesale lenders provide faster approvals and wider loan selection.

Government Involvement in Real Estate Financing

Federal and local government entities actively shape real estate financing through varied policies, programs, and oversight. From FHA backing to Fed interest moves the public sector exerts considerable influence on lending markets. Savvy real estate professionals stay abreast of key government measures affecting financing to best counsel clients and forecast trends.

FHA Mortgage Insurance

The Federal Housing Administration (FHA) insures approved lenders against losses on qualifying mortgages. This expanded home financing after the Great Depression. FHA requirements standardize industry norms for documentation, debt ratios, and appraisals. FHA mortgages ease access for moderate-income and first-time buyers. Changes to FHA policies significantly sway mortgage availability.

Fannie Mae and Freddie Mac

These government-sponsored enterprises (GSEs) power secondary mortgage markets by purchasing mortgages from lenders to provide fresh lending capital. Conforming loans adhering to Fannie/Freddie standards are widely available, given their robust secondary market. Policy adjustments by the GSEs can loosen or tighten overall financing.

Federal Reserve Actions

The Federal Reserve influences real estate financing dramatically through monetary policy. Lower Fed interest rates spur lending and home sales while hikes cool markets. Quantitative easing by the Fed impacts availability indirectly by stimulating lending activity. Real estate professionals should grasp Fed powers and follow key interest decisions.

Dodd-Frank Act

Passed after the subprime mortgage crisis, Dodd-Frank imposed sweeping reforms on real estate financing regulation. It created the Consumer Financial Protection Bureau (CFPB) to oversee lenders and protect borrowers while mandating stricter lending standards. Dodd-Frank affects mortgage processes and disclosures.

State and Local Regulation

State and local governments also regulate real estate financing through license requirements, disclosure laws, banking department oversight, and industry statutes. Municipal grant and second mortgage programs may also assist local home purchases. Real estate professionals should be well-informed about state/local measures affecting real estate deals.

Loan Application Process and Procedures

Guiding buyers through mortgage loan applications represents a core real estate service. Professionals should have in-depth command of the documentation, assessment, underwriting, and approval steps within the application process to set realistic client expectations while ensuring smooth financing. This section outlines key phases and technical knowledge for successfully managing the mortgage process.

Required Documentation

Loan applications require extensive financial documentation, including paystubs, tax returns, bank statements, existing property records, and more. Helping clients prepare these in advance streamlines approval. Key disclosures acknowledge receiving legal notifications per TILA and RESPA. Documentation organization is vital for mortgage processing.

Property Appraisal and Financing Contingencies

Lender-ordered appraisals verify property value to size loans appropriately. Preapproval letters make financing contingent on acceptable appraisal. Real estate professionals must educate buyers that low appraisals may require a renegotiating price or securing additional capital. Contingencies provide flexibility if financing falls through.

Loan Underwriting and Credit Scoring

Mortgage lenders scrutinize applications through underwriting to assess default statistical risk with extensive financial modeling. Credit scores factor heavily in determining the offered interest rates. Real estate agents should help buyers optimize credit and DTI ratios ahead of underwriting to strengthen approvals.

Loan Approval Conditions

Final mortgage approvals often carry restrictive conditions. Borrowers may need to pay off debts, provide updated income verification right before closing, or fund escrow accounts. Professionals should inform clients of typical approval stipulations and limitations to avoid last-minute surprises. Meeting conditions ensures funding disbursal.

Closing Process Coordination

Agents often assist with closing logistics like final walkthroughs, disbursals, and coordinating documents and attendees. Staying organized and reviewing closing documents in advance helps identify any lingering issues before the closing appointment for smooth finalization. Knowledge of closing procedures proves invaluable.

Alternative Financing Strategies

Besides standard mortgages, real estate professionals should also maintain awareness of alternative financing like seller financing, lease options, crowdfunding, private loans, and real estate partnerships. In certain cases, creativity may be required to fund deals. Understanding multiple financing avenues provides professionals with more options to explore with buyers.

Chapter 4: Valuation and Market Analysis

Determining accurate property valuations and monitoring market conditions represent core real estate professional duties. Through appraisals and comparative market analyses (CMAs), agents quantify intrinsic home values based on characteristics like size, age, and condition. Tracking supply/demand metrics, sales data, and macroeconomic forces offers critical insight into the state of local real estate markets. This chapter covers essential property appraisal methods, value influences, CMA elements, indicators of market strength or weakness, and the interplay between property-specific and market-wide factors. Future success depends on the expertise in valuation and market analytics.

Principles of Value

Several key principles form the theoretical foundation for real estate valuation. Understanding these concepts allows professionals to fully comprehend factors impacting worth when performing appraisals and counseling clients. From the economic forces that shape value to various depreciation types, this section provides a robust grounding in value theory.

Market Value

The fair market value of a property represents the most probable price it would command in a competitive market between informed buyers and sellers acting prudently. This excludes distressed or forced sales and considers the property's highest and best legal use. Real estate professionals must know market value parameters for accurate pricing.

Substitution, Balance, and Contribution

The principle of substitution holds that a buyer will not pay a higher amount for a property than the cost of acquiring an equivalent substitute property. The balance principle states that property value depends on the equilibrium between supply and demand for property type. The contribution principle bases value on how much net income the property generates.

Depreciation Types

Depreciation reduces property value due to physical deterioration, functional obsolescence, or external economic factors. Physical depreciation involves natural wear. Functional depreciation results from outdated designs. External depreciation can occur due to local market declines. Professionals should factor in all depreciation types when appraising.

Special Value Considerations

Some buyers assign special value to properties for personal reasons or anticipated improvements. For example, commercial zoning holds added value for a buyer planning conversion from residential use. Real estate professionals must recognize when special considerations merit value premiums.

Remaining Economic Life

The remaining economic life estimates how many years the property can continue generating income or satisfaction before becoming obsolete. The depreciation rate and effective age determine the remaining economic life. Newer properties with many useful years remaining hold higher values.

Property Appraisal Methods

Professional appraisers utilize three main valuation methods - cost, sales comparison, and income capitalization approaches. Each analyzes distinct factors to derive property values. While appraisers weigh all methods, understanding each provides invaluable insight for even preliminary valuation guidance. This section outlines the key elements of the three methods.

Cost Approach

The cost approach sums the land value and costs to reproduce or replace the improvements minus accrued depreciation. The land value may use sales comps of vacant lots. Improvement costs are estimated via replacement or reproduction costs and then adjusted for accumulated depreciation types. Buyers hardly pay the full cost, so this method has limited utility alone.

Sales Comparison Approach

This common method compares recent sales of similar properties to find value. Adjustments are made for property differences, including age, size, condition, location, and features. When local comparable sales are abundant, this method carries significant weight in reconciling the final appraised value. Real estate professionals rely heavily on sales comparison in comparative market analyses.

Income Capitalization Approach

Commercial properties are often valued based on income-generating potential. This approach capitalizes net operating income via an overall capitalization rate:

Value = Net Operating Income / Capitalization Rate.

It converts future cash flows into an indication of current value. Capitalization rates derive from market sales comps. Real estate professionals utilize this method for rental and commercial valuations.

Reconciliation of Value Indications

The appraiser weighs the relative merits of each approach and methodology, given the local market and property type. Reconciliation combines the separate value indications into a final opinion of value. Real estate agents can provide better pricing guidance by understanding how appraisers synthesize different valuations in a reconciliation.

Market Analysis Techniques

In addition to valuation, real estate professionals must track key market indicators to identify existing conditions and future trends. Through careful market analysis, agents provide clients with critical price guidance anchored in economic fundamentals rather than guesswork. This section covers compiling comparable sales, monitoring supply/demand dynamics, and studying market metrics.

Selecting Comp Sale Properties

Comparable sales reports analyze recently sold properties similar to the subject for pricing insights. Ideal comps are nearby, recent, and alike in physical characteristics, usage, and market segment. Adjustments account for differences. Real estate professionals should select the best 3-5 comps with logical adjustments when developing sales comparisons and CMAs.

Monitoring Supply and Demand

The balance between real estate supply and demand can have a significant impact on prices. When supply is short, prices often rise in a seller's market. Oversupply creates a buyers' market. Real estate professionals track listing counts, days on the market, and sale-to-list ratios to gauge supply/demand balance, to adjust pricing.

Absorption Rate and Marketing Time

The absorption rate measures the number of sales per month relative to active listings. Marketing time calculates the average number of days properties spend on the market before selling. These metrics indicate buyer demand and ideal listing prices to meet market realities. Professionals should study absorption and marketing times.

Leading Economic Indicators

Housing follows the overall economy. Key leading indicators to watch include GDP, unemployment, consumer confidence, mortgage rates, building permits, and housing starts. Real estate professionals who monitor these macroeconomic factors can better forecast market shifts and position clients for success.

Demographic Trends

Ongoing demographic changes impact real estate markets, especially household formation and migration to/from a region. Interest rate impacts also differ across age brackets. Savvy professionals analyze evolving demographic trends to identify promising market segments and demand drivers.

Chapter 5: Contracts

In the world of real estate, contracts are the backbone of nearly every transaction. They lay out key terms, conditions, rights, and responsibilities that guide the deal from inception through closing. For real estate professionals, a deep understanding of contracts is imperative. This chapter will provide a comprehensive overview of contracts, including different types and key clauses, elements required for a valid contract, implications of breaches, and remedies available. With a firm grasp of contracts, real estate agents can expertly guide clients, ensure their interests are protected, and avoid potentially costly mistakes.

Types of Real Estate Contracts

Real estate transactions utilize a variety of specific contract types depending on factors, such as the property type, transaction purpose, and number of parties involved. Here, we will explore some of the most common contracts real estate professionals must understand to do their job efficiently.

Purchase and Sale Agreements

Also known as real estate purchase agreements or real estate sales contracts, these outline the terms for the transfer of property ownership between a buyer and seller. They detail critical information like the property description, sale price, deposit amount, contingencies, closing date, and more. Purchase and sale agreements form the crux of most real estate transactions, governing the entire process from offer to receiving the keys.

Leases

Lease agreements delineate the rights and obligations of landlords and tenants in rental arrangements. Key details include the property description, rent amount and due date, lease term, security deposit, use of premises, maintenance and repairs, insurance requirements, and termination provisions. Leases underpin most landlord-tenant relationships and can be for any type of property, from apartments to single-family homes, retail spaces, or offices.

Options to Purchase

Also referred to as option contracts, these give a potential buyer the right, but not the obligation, to buy a property within a specific timeframe in exchange for consideration. The option agreement sets key terms like the purchase price, option consideration amount, option period, and procedures for exercise. Options provide flexibility to buyers while allowing sellers to retain backup offers. Common in new construction, options enable buyers to delay purchases until project completion.

Offers to Purchase

Buyers use offers to purchase to present proposed terms to a seller for the acquisition of real estate. While not binding contracts themselves, signed offers represent serious intent to buy if accepted. Offers outline the proposed price, desired closing date, amount of earnest money deposit, contingencies, and other terms. If accepted by the seller, the offer forms the basis for crafting a subsequent purchase agreement. Offers are commonly used by buyers to start negotiations.

Commercial Leases

These long-term rental contracts govern the landlord-tenant relationship in commercial real estate for properties like retail spaces, office buildings, and industrial facilities. Details include identification of parties, property description, permitted commercial use, rent terms, maintenance responsibilities, improvements, insurance obligations, and termination clauses. Commercial leases may also contain options to renew or purchase. Thorough understanding helps real estate agents expertly represent clients.

Residential Leases

Residential leases set terms for landlords, providing tenants with habitation rights in return for rent payments. Key details include property description, occupant names, lease duration, amount due, payment frequency, security deposit, use restrictions, maintenance and repairs, whether smoking, pets, and guests are permitted, as well as termination requirements. Many jurisdictions require specific landlord-tenant disclosures. Residential leases underlie the rental housing market, governing relationships between tenants and owners of apartments, houses, and condos.

Short-Term Rental Agreements

Like residential leases, short-term rental agreements outline terms for temporary stays. Used for vacation rentals and other short-duration lodging, details include property description, rental term, rate and taxes, security deposit, cancellation policy, check-in/check-out times, rules of occupancy, and signature lines. Clear terms help ensure positive experiences for both owners and guests. Real estate agents may assist clients on both sides of short-term rental deals.

Escrow Agreements

Escrow agreements authorize a neutral third party to hold assets on behalf of transacting parties until certain conditions are met. In real estate, earnest money deposits are often held in escrow accounts. Escrow agreements outline conditions like inspection contingencies to be met before releasing funds. They provide an intermediary layer of security between contract signing and closing. Real estate agents routinely interact with escrow companies.

Key Contract Terms and Clauses

Offer and Acceptance

Fundamentally, a valid contract requires an offer and corresponding acceptance. Real estate deals commence with an offer presented to a prospective seller outlining the proposed purchase terms. If the seller accepts the offer, expressly or through conduct, a contract exists. Agents must recognize clear offers and acceptance to assess a contract's validity and enforceability. Offers not explicitly accepted may only represent negotiations.

Identification of Parties

Contracts must identify the names of the buyer and seller. Full legal names establish who the contractual parties are. Correct identification also enables checking backgrounds, titles, and financing ability. For residential sales, inquiries like marital status help determine rights and obligations. Accurately identifying parties is essential.

Property Description

Thorough property descriptions establish the real estate involved. Full address and parcel numbers precisely identify the property. Further details like square footage, bedrooms, acreage, outbuildings, or amenities ensure both parties understand exactly what is being transacted. Insufficient descriptions create ambiguity, undermining enforcement.

Price and Deposit

The purchase price and amount of earnest money deposit detail the terms of the sales. The price anchors negotiations, while the deposit shows the buyer's good faith. Payment methods and the handling of deposits should be clearly articulated. Reasonable deposits are typically held in escrow until closing. Agents must ensure the price and deposit terms are clear.

Closing Provisions

Closing procedures address the pivotal exchange of property rights for payment. This includes identifying the closing company, specifying documents to be furnished, allocating costs like title fees, and establishing the closing date. Setting an outside closing date protects parties if difficulties arise. The handling of closing procedures should be addressed upfront with both parties.

Possession Parameters

Possession details like date and time guide the property handover. Buyers want access as soon as possible, while sellers may need time to vacate. Occupancy rights should be explicit, especially if sellers retain temporary possession. Pre-closing walkthroughs, therefore, may be arranged. Clear possession parameters prevent potential misunderstandings.

Contingencies

Contingencies spell out conditions that must be fulfilled before the parties' performance obligations kick in. Real estate contingencies that can commonly come up include financing, appraisal, inspection, and title contingencies. Buyers do not want to be obligated unless mortgage, value, condition, and title issues are clearly addressed. Sellers may counteroffer to limit contingency scope or duration as an incentive.

Obligations of Parties

The duties of buyers and sellers should be clear throughout the transaction. Buyers may need to promptly apply for financing and make inspections within strict time frames. Sellers must provide a clear title and maintain the property. Agents depend on both parties' clarity of obligations in order to appropriately counsel clients.

Risk of Loss Provision

This clause addresses responsibility if property damage occurs between contract signing and closing. Generally, the risk remains with the seller until the title transfers but it can shift earlier. Agents must recognize the risk of loss implications when events like fire or extreme weather damage occur. Customized risk-of-loss clauses may be negotiated.

Default Conditions

Default clauses outline contractual breaches that relieve injured parties of performance responsibility while often allowing them to pursue remedies. Monetary defaults like nonpayment and situational defaults like misrepresentation should be set forth. Default provisions vary but always address nonperformance.

Boilerplate Terms

Boilerplate terms cover standard legal matters like severability, survival, notice procedures, rules of construction, waiver, governing law, and signature lines. While often glossed over, issues like which state's laws govern interpretation can be crucial. Agents should recognize standard boilerplate terms.

Contract Breaches

A contract breach occurs when one party fails to satisfy its agreed obligations without legal excuse. Breaches run from technical violations like paying rent late to material failures such as the inability to deliver marketable titles at closing. Determining whether a minor or major breach exists is key for remedies.

Material vs. Minor Breaches

Minor technical breaches may not discharge other parties' duty to perform if they still receive the expected substantial benefit. Drastic failures depriving parties of expected value constitute material breaches, excusing their obligations. Severity, not simplicity, determines materiality. Nonperformance, not slight deviation from the obligation, causes discharge.

Actual vs. Anticipatory Breaches

Actual breaches occur when a contract duty goes unfulfilled, like failing to close. Anticipatory breaches arise pre-performance when a party unequivocally signals inability or unwillingness to perform. If a seller says they have sold to another buyer, the initial one may have anticipatory breach rights despite the initial closing date not having arrived yet.

Partial vs. Total Breaches

Total breaches entail the complete failure of an entire performance obligation, destroying contractual value. Partial breaches occur when essential duties are performed poorly or not at all. Sellers providing a house but not conveying adjacent land as agreed have partially breached. In real estate, most material breaches are total.

Waiver of Contract Breaches

If a party knows of a breach but continues to accept performance or acts inconsistently with the breach, they implicitly waive the right to recover. Buyers who are close to knowing of title defects may waive rights. However, waivers for future breaches do not exist. Waiver analysis is very fact-specific.

Subsequent Breaches

Previous breaches by one party do not justify future breaches by the injured party. Buyers who close on a home after discovering defects cannot just stop mortgage payments. Performance remains required even after the other party's uncured material breaches.

Burden of Proof

The injured party bears the burden of proving a breach exists. Evidence must demonstrate failure of agreed contractual duty. This includes producing the contract, breached provisions, supporting documentation, and proof of resultant harm. Verdicts can hinge on the plaintiff's ability to prove breach elements.

Contract Remedies

Damages

Monetary damages provide compensation for losses caused by a breach. Buyers deprived of expected appreciation or sellers with carrying costs may recover damages. Mathematical precision is not required, but the loss must be reasonably established and causally connected. Speculative future damages, however, are not recoverable.

Specific Performance

This equitable remedy requires the delivery of goods or performance as agreed in the contract. Specific performance is commonly sought to compel the conveyance of real estate rather than only damages. It is generally available unless impractical or inadequate. Sellers may obtain specific performance if buyers default.

Rescission

Rescission cancels the contract, unwinding it as if never made. Available for some fraudulent or breaching acts, rescission restores pre-contract status. Buyers might seek rescission and refund if sellers deliberately concealed defects. Rescission may require tendering back what was received.

Reformation

Reformation corrects inaccuracies in the contract, like transcription errors, to reflect the true intent of the parties. If a lease term was written as 9 years instead of the agreed 90 years, reformation can amend the error. Reformation requires clear evidence of mistakes thwarting intent.

Liquidated Damages

Parties may agree upfront on set damage amounts for certain breaches. A seller might require a $50 per day retention of possession past closing. Liquidated damages must be a reasonable estimate and not punitive. Excessive amounts may be unenforceable.

Chapter 6: Agency Relationships and Practices

Navigating the complex world of real estate transactions requires a deep understanding of agency relationships. At the heart of every property deal lies the dynamic between buyers, sellers, and their agents. This chapter provides you with a robust exploration of how agency connections are formed, the fiduciary duties binding agents, and the vital need for proper disclosures.

Creation and Termination of Agency

Agency relationships serve as the foundation for interactions between clients and real estate professionals. This section examines the establishment, scope, and dissolution of these connections in detail. From express written agreements to implied affiliations, we will tackle the nuances of agency creation. You will also gain insight into termination, from expiration to revocation, along with the procedures for properly severing ties.

Agency Basics

Real estate transactions intrinsically rely on agents faithfully representing their client's interests. Agency relationships facilitate this by contractually binding professionals to certain duties. But how exactly is agency established? There are several key ways connections are created between agents and clients.

Express agency agreements constitute the most straightforward means. These are written contracts directly detailing the agent's representation of a buyer or seller. Generally, express agreements explicitly spell out the rights and responsibilities of both parties involved. They provide clear documentation of representation for a defined period or transaction.

The agency can also stem from oral agreements made verbally between an agent and buyer or seller. Through spoken conversation, both parties consent to the agent representing the client's interests regarding a property transaction. However, oral agreements can lack concrete details on scope or duration. Having agency terms clearly documented in writing is generally recommended.

In some cases, agency relationships can be implied based on the circumstances and conduct between parties. For instance, a buyer who repeatedly relies on an agent's assistance when viewing potential properties could be considered an implied client. If an agent continuously looks out for a seller's interests during negotiations, this suggests implied agency.

The agency can also be created through ratification. This occurs when a customer accepts an agent's previously unauthorized actions, essentially retroactively granting them representative powers. Suppose an agent mistakenly believes they represent a seller, yet the seller later endorses their transaction efforts. This ratification confirms an agency relationship existed.

Agency Scope and Duties

Real estate agent's responsibilities directly correspond to the scope of their representation. The type and extent of an agency relationship fundamentally impact the agent's role and legal obligations.

For sellers, agency relationships generally fall under two main categories:

- Exclusive seller agency: The brokerage and agent represent the seller exclusively. This bars them from concurrently representing buyers interested in the seller's property.
- Open seller agency: The brokerage represents the seller, but individual agents can also work with buyers, becoming dual agents. This allows greater flexibility but can present conflicts.

For buyers, there are also two primary agency categories:

- Exclusive buyer agency: The brokerage and agent solely represent the buyer's interests. They cannot simultaneously represent any sellers the buyer wishes to conduct transactions with.
- Non-exclusive buyer agency: The brokerage represents the buyer, but agents are not prohibited from also representing sellers as dual agents if needed. This provides more flexibility but also entails managing conflicts.

Beyond formal representation, real estate professionals also assist ordinary customers who have not established expressed agency connections. Certain basic duties still apply, including honesty, disclosure, confidentiality, and reasonable care. However, customers do not receive full fiduciary obligations.

Creation Formalities

Finalizing an express agency agreement requires adhering to key formalities. This officially documented process binds both agent and client to the relationship's terms and conditions.

In most states, agency contracts must be in writing to be enforceable. Oral agreements can be considered non-binding. All express agreements should prominently specify that an agency affiliation is being established. Additionally, details on scope, compensation, and duration of representation should be included.

Signatures from both the agent and client are generally required to authorize the agreement. In some states, the agent must have an active real estate license to create a valid agency relationship. E-signatures are usually acceptable, but parties should check regulations to ensure compliance.

Legally, agency agreements do not require an end date and can allow for open-ended representation. However, contracts usually establish parameters for the relationship's natural expiration. Common expiration triggers include completing a specific transaction, a set date on the calendar arriving, or either party terminates the affiliation.

Disclosed Dual Agency

In certain transactions, a brokerage may act as a dual agent representing both buyers and sellers. This creates special disclosure requirements.

Dual agency arises when an agent representing a buyer has colleagues at the same brokerage firm representing the seller. This situation presents an inherent conflict of interest; no professional can solely look out for two opposing parties simultaneously.

Thus, dual agency is only permitted if all parties provide informed written consent. This disclosure verifies that clients understand the divided loyalties a dual agency creates. Most states prohibit dual agents from advocating exclusively for one party over the other. They must remain neutral, only facilitating the transaction.

Strict confidentiality is crucial for dual agents. Details about either client can generally not be revealed or used to benefit the other party. Dual agents tend to have a more limited negotiating capacity compared to sole client representation. Clients should comprehend these constraints before consenting.

Termination Procedures

Just as formalities create an agency, specific procedures must be followed to terminate relationships. Understanding these proper methods for dissolving agencies is essential for practicing real estate professionals.

Express written agreements often stipulate expiration conditions, serving as natural termination points. Common triggers include a set date of arrival, a property closing, or either party providing notification. It is important to review contracts carefully to anticipate when representation formally ends.

For open-ended agreements, either the agent or client can terminate unilaterally through written notice. Reasonable notice periods are customary for terminations without cause, while breach of contract or misrepresentation are common grounds for immediate termination. States may dictate required termination procedures as well.

Duties and Responsibilities of Agents

Real estate agents assume significant legal and ethical duties upon representing buyers and sellers. This section details these extensive fiduciary obligations. You will examine the varied responsibilities tied to loyalty, disclosure, accounting, and reasonable care. Appreciating the gravity of an agent's role is vital for anyone pursuing real estate as a profession.

Loyalty and Obedience

An agent's primary duty is demonstrating loyalty to their client through obedient service. As fiduciaries, real estate professionals must act solely in their client's best interests. This obligation outweighs the agent's personal interests in all matters related to the represented transaction.

Clients expect faithful loyalty from their agents. This means following all legal instructions, providing honest, competent counsel, as well as proactively informing them of any material information that could impact decisions. If a seller instructs their agent to reject offers below the asking price, obediently adhering to those wishes is essential.

While duties obviously extend to buyers and sellers in agency relationships, certain obligations also exist when working with non-client customers. Reasonable care, honesty, and disclosure of material facts must still be practiced. However, customers receive less comprehensive loyalty than actual clients.

Skill and Competency

Alongside loyalty, real estate agents owe clients the duty to provide skilled, competent services. This requires agents to have command of all critical areas related to properties and transactions.

Specifically, agents need expertise in:

- Property valuations and pricing guidance
- Market conditions research
- Advertising and property exposure tactics
- Negotiation strategies and facilitation
- Purchase agreement and contract preparation
- Available financing/lending options
- Earnest money processing and procedures
- Regional zoning regulations
- Property disclosures and inspection protocols
- Title search and due diligence facilitation
- Closing document preparation and execution

Staying continually updated on the latest laws, regulations, and real estate trends is crucial for providing competent service. Clients depend on agents' know-how.

Reasonable Care and Diligence

Exercising reasonable care and diligence represents another key fiduciary duty. Real estate agents must utilize their skills and resources prudently to secure their client's best interests.

For sellers, this includes thoroughly assessing a property's value, actively marketing to suitable buyers, skillfully screening and vetting offers, and adequately preparing closing documents. Buyer's agents need to locate optimal properties, arrange showings, oversee inspections, ensure clear title, and avoid unnecessary delays. Guiding clients through negotiations further demonstrates reasonable care.

Promoting the client's interests with professionalism and urgency while avoiding careless oversights indicates reasonable diligence. Savvy knowledge and follow-through are imperative. Accepting anything less violates an agent's fiduciary duty.

Confidentiality

Keeping sensitive client information fully confidential constitutes another central real estate agent's responsibility. As fiduciaries, agents must exercise utmost discretion and never disclose details that could compromise their client's interests.

Confidential information includes any personal or financial details related to the client. It also encompasses the client's bargaining position and motivations. For sellers specifically, the lowest acceptable price is confidential. For buyers, the highest price they are willing to offer is not for sharing.

Dual agents face particular confidentiality challenges. They cannot reveal insights learned from one client to benefit the other. Strict confidentiality and informed consent help mitigate conflicts in dual-agency scenarios. However, the greater challenge of solely protecting information remains.

Full Disclosure

While preserving a client's confidentiality is crucial, agents also bear the duty of full disclosure to their clients. Any material facts that could influence the client's decisions must be promptly communicated.

Material facts encompass information like offers received, knowledge of defects, competitive listings, and market trends. While some disclosure requirements vary by state, open communication that facilitates informed decision-making is universally expected.

Disclosure should occur the moment pertinent information becomes accessible. The most diligent agents go beyond just reacting to mandatory disclosure laws and proactively provide any details that could impact their client's interests. They understand that readily volunteering crucial information exemplifies their duty.

Promotion of the Client's Interests

As fiduciaries, real estate agents must strive at all times to promote their clients' best interests. This supersedes any self-interested motivations an agent may have. Sometimes, promotion obligations manifest through counsel and advice. Agents may need to tactfully inform sellers when over-pricing a property or make buyers aware of more ideal options. Other times, promotion involves negotiations. Representing a buyer's best interests could mean counseling them to increase an offer. Or agents may need to persuade sellers to lower excessive expectations.

While never misrepresenting, effective agents understand that different situations call for different promotional tactics. But the constant is prioritizing the client's interests above all else. This defines an agent's purpose.

Accounting for Funds

As monetary transactions are central to real estate deals, proper handling of finances is imperative. Meticulously accounting for all money held for clients provides essential transparency and protection. From earnest money deposits to equity proceeds, agents must keep detailed records of funds received and disbursed. Earnest monies need particular care, as agents serve as neutral third-party holders. Precise tracking and timely distribution upon closing are vital.

Some states require separate client trust accounts for real estate funds. Agents may want to consider them regardless, as this separation provides helpful transparency. Accurate record-keeping, including written receipts and monthly statements, aids reliable accounting. It also helps agents avoid confusion when managing money for multiple clients.

Agent Representation and Disclosures

Real estate agents navigate a complex web of relationships with buyers, sellers, and their brokerages. Given potential conflicts, both agents and brokerages must make key disclosures that illuminate their roles. This promotes transparency and protects clients. This section examines the representations made by agents and the mandatory disclosures surrounding them. You will tackle topics ranging from self-dealings to agency membership.

Licensed Status

Real estate agents must disclose that they are licensed professionals representing clients' interests. This status separates them from non-licensed salespeople.

In promoting or discussing properties, licensed agents must expressly represent themselves as licensed professionals, not ordinary sellers. All marketing materials, business cards, and documents should indicate licensure. Verbally disclosing licensed status when meeting potential clients provides further clarity.

Explicitly presenting oneself as a licensed agent affords legal authority to facilitate transactions. It also signifies adherence to ethical duties. Consumers have a right to know an agent's credentials and obligations. Omitting licensure disclosure can constitute illegal misrepresentation.

Brokerage Affiliation

Real estate agents must transparently disclose their affiliated brokerage firm. Licenses alone do not allow agents to practice; they must be attached to a brokerage's license and work under its supervision.

Listings, contracts, and marketing materials should prominently indicate the brokerage an agent is associated with. Verbally disclosing brokerage affiliation also breeds familiarity and trust with consumers. This opens the door to developing new business relationships.

Omitting brokerage information constitutes misrepresentation. Furthermore, failing to disclose brokerage ties would obscure that the firm and designated broker bear responsibility for the agent's conduct. Consumers have a right to understand exactly who stands behind an agent.

Agency Relationships

Disclosures regarding agency status provide clients with transparent insights into existing and potential affiliations. This allows consumers to make informed decisions.

In engaging with new clients, agents need to clarify whom they presently represent and how they can or cannot represent other parties. Explicitly stating if they already have a buyer's or seller's agreement in place or can freely enter into one with new customers allows alignment of expectations.

When dealing with unrepresented customers, simply stating no formal agency connection currently exists defines the relationship clearly. Agents should additionally explain available representation options that could establish an official affiliation. However, they cannot speak or negotiate directly with customers without consent.

Dual Agency

When simultaneously representing a buyer and seller, thorough dual agency disclosures become mandatory. This informs all parties of the inherent conflicts at play.

A dual agent cannot satisfy one client's objectives without potentially harming the others. Necessary disclosures make clients aware of dual agents' restricted negotiating abilities and the burdens imposed in keeping confidences. This allows clients to willingly consent to such compromised representation or seek alternatives.

State laws dictate the precise due process for authorizing dual agency. However, comprehensive written disclosures and signed consent agreements are universal requirements. Ambiguous dual agent loyalties demand extra transparency.

Self-Dealings

Rigorous disclosure requirements govern any financial transactions in which real estate agents have a personal stake. Self-dealings warrant heightened scrutiny.

Agents are obligated to promptly disclose any self-interests in their client's transactions. Ownership or entanglements with lenders, inspectors, contractors, or other parties connected to an agent's client dealings must become known. This revelation allows clients to objectively assess how the affiliation could skew objectivity.

Commonly, states prohibit agents from acting in dual-agent capacities in self-dealing scenarios without explicit approval. Agents may face strict penalties for concealed ties. Compromised objectivity conflicts with an agent's duties. Thus, any personal stakes require forthright admissions.

Outside Expertise

Real estate agents may involve various affiliated professionals like lenders, home inspectors, or contractors to facilitate transactions. Working with known expert associates can benefit clients. However, affiliation disclosures remain key.

When referring clients to any allied professionals, agents need transparency regarding their regular working relationship. This informs consumers so they do not assume false impartiality but rather see recommendations as tied to the agent's network.

Disclosures should indicate that customers maintain full freedom to use unaffiliated professionals at their discretion. However, agents can highlight the benefits of working with their familiar expert contacts. As long as they disclose associations, agents can build trust through dependable support networks.

Chapter 7: General Real Estate Practices

Day-to-day operations form the lifeblood of thriving real estate practices. From listing properties to nurturing ethical conduct, this chapter delves into the critical tasks and responsibilities entailed in the field. You will gain insights into the listing and selling processes that build successful businesses. Standards for professional behavior provide guidance on nurturing integrity and public trust. Methods for recognizing and mitigating risk offer prudent protections when managing vulnerable transactions. Altogether, absorbing this content will equip you to steer daily real estate workflows with proficiency.

Listing and Selling Process

The listing and selling of properties encompass the fundamental real estate transactions driving professionals' livelihoods. Let's unpack these intricate processes, from initial consultations to closing. You will gain an understanding of listing agreements, showing procedures, offer strategies, negotiating, financing, inspections, appraisals, and closing preparations. Grasping the many moving parts of buying and selling properties provides the foundational knowledge to facilitate smooth transactions.

Listing Appointments

Productive listing appointments set the stage for securing new business by converting promising seller leads into committed clients.

Effective listing presentations accomplish three key goals: establishing rapport and trust with potential clients, assessing the subject property thoroughly, and conveying the agent's credentials and value proposition. Blending educational and promotional elements requires thoughtful balance and attentive listening skills to understand the client's needs.

Common elements to cover include: competitive market analyses, estimated pricing guidance, proposed listing terms, customized marketing plans, agent/brokerage qualifications, transaction management services, and commission/fee structures. Handouts and visual aids help convey information clearly. The ultimate aim is securing an executed listing agreement.

Listing Agreements

Listing agreements formalize the contract granting a brokerage exclusive right to sell a property during a defined period. These legally binding documents detail essential terms guiding the listing relationship.

Key components include the listed price, permitted brokerage compensation, length of agreement, and brokerage obligations regarding marketing and facilitation efforts. Also specified are conditions allowing the brokerage to alter the asking price, accept backup offers, and share commissions with cooperating brokerages. Owners reserve the right to procure their own buyers without paying commissions in most agreements.

Finalizing listing contracts requires owners' informed consent. Agents must explain all terms and gain signatures. Modifying or extending existing listing agreements similarly requires a mutual written agreement. Proper documentation prevents misunderstandings.

Marketing and Showings

The marketing period following a listing agreement's execution vitally frames buyers' initial impressions of a property. Savvy marketing and liberal showing availability boost visibility.

Recommended marketing elements include:

High-quality listing photos/videos conveying appeal; compelling descriptions are accentuating amenities/upgrades; targeted online ads through MLS and social media platforms; print signage and flyers drawing neighborhood attention; open houses for increased exposure and fielding feedback; email blasts to potentially interested parties in the agent's sphere of influence; and strategic outreach to likely buyers primed for properties' attributes.

Accommodating buyer agents' showing requests readily, along with availability for public open houses, helps properties stand out. Proactive efforts to nurture buyer enthusiasm, maximize sales potential. But client guidance on showing preparation, optimizes impressions.

Offer Strategies and Negotiations

Securing fair, favorable offers requires planning and skill. Counseling sellers on offer strategies tailored to market conditions provide an edge.

In seller's markets with high demand, pricing competitively generates multiple offers. This allows for leveraging bidding wars and inflated bids. Alternatively, setting fixed prices works better in balanced markets with moderate demand. In buyer's markets, pricing below value incites urgency and bidding activity at an affordable level.

Handling negotiations also necessitates strategic considerations. Reasonable counteroffers maintain deal momentum while still advancing sellers' interests. Savvy agents advise clients on where pricing concessions make sense and how to strengthen terms or extract buyer contributions. They focus negotiations on creating the greatest value for sellers.

Purchase Offers

Purchase offers formally indicate buyers' interest in properties and proposed deal terms. Receiving, reviewing, and responding to these constitutes another core real estate activity.

Agents must present all purchase offers to sellers for consideration immediately. They should then provide objective insights on terms based on market dynamics and the property itself. Comparable sales and appraisal data help assess the reasonability of listed prices versus offered amounts.

Sellers decide whether to accept offers, reject them, or counter them with adjusted terms. Purchase contracts do not legally bind sellers until signed and delivered. Agents assist with drafting strategic counteroffers designed to keep deals progressing favorably.

Financing Contingencies

Most real estate purchase offers contain financing contingencies, allowing buyers to cancel contracts if suitable mortgages fail to materialize. Savvy agents proactively address these terms.

They verify buyers are prequalified with lenders, examine deals' loan-to-value ratios, and confirm that the included terms will satisfy underwriting requirements. Agents may also push for shorter financing contingency windows to prevent drawn-out delays.

If deals face mortgage denials, extending contingency deadlines or renegotiating terms can potentially salvage transactions. But contingency removal adds closing pressures on buyers. Agents must balance both buyer and seller interests thoughtfully when navigating financing.

Home Inspections

Facilitating property inspections helps transactions proceed based on objective information. Agents schedule visits, oversee assessments and manage resultant negotiations.

They help educate buyers on inspection scope and make sellers aware of common issues that may surface. If defects arise, agents can obtain contractor estimates for buyers to gauge remediation costs in considering price concessions.

However, agents also need to mediate excessive buyer demands and unreasonable seller objections. The ultimate goal is achieving mutual satisfaction, with parties agreeing on any repairs, credits, or lowered prices warranted by inspection findings. Reasoned compromises keep deals viable.

Title Reports and Surveys

Title reports and boundary surveys likewise provide objective transaction data, revealing any property title or boundary defects needing remediation.

Title reports disclose past conveyances, encumbrances such as liens, and other recorded matters impacting title. Surveys map legal boundaries and building setbacks while pinpointing structural encroachments.

Agents review these reports, relaying any red flags to the appropriate parties. They may advise legal counsel when title clarity or boundary issues seem insoluble. However, the goal remains securing clean title conveyance and uncontested boundaries for a smooth closing.

Appraisals

Lender-ordered appraisals protect buyers by substantiating that purchase prices reflect fair market value. However, low values threaten deals. Skilled agents proactively address appraisal concerns.

They lay the groundwork, ensuring appraisers understand all property enhancements and favorable market conditions, boosting value. If initial appraisals still miss the mark, agents can request reconsideration while providing supplementary valuation data for support.

Price renegotiations present another option if gaps with appraised values appear insurmountable. However, reasonable appraiser engagement helps avoid this undesirable outcome.

Closing Preparations

Myriad details require attention as transactions approach closing. Agents adeptly coordinate these final staging steps.

They ensure all documents are signed and collected, oversee final walkthroughs, arrange utility transfers, and verify closing costs and prorations. Receiving purchase funds, dispensing commission checks, and finalizing ownership transfers also fall under agent duties leading up to this climactic transaction milestone.

Attentive agents even handle small yet meaningful gestures like providing clients with gift baskets at closing. Orchestrating a smooth, stress-free closing experience demonstrates an agent's reliability.

Ethics and Professional Behavior

Maintaining rigorous standards of ethics and professionalism allows real estate practitioners to earn public trust and protect clients. This section examines the codes of conduct governing agents along with principles for exemplary professional behavior. We will explore common ethical dilemmas and best practices for principled decision-making. Mastering these ethical foundations prepares you for the moral and behavioral rigors of this relationship-driven field.

Professional Certification

Voluntary professional certifications signify an agent's commitment to ethics and expertise. Credential programs establish standards of knowledge, conduct, and accountability that distinguish members from average licensees.

The National Association of REALTORS'® REALTOR® designation is America's largest credential. REALTORS® must complete training, pay dues, and adhere to the group's Code of Ethics. Membership signals adherence to rigorous standards.

Other prominent examples include the Certified Real Estate Brokerage Manager (CRB) for brokers and the Accredited Buyer's Representative (ABR) for buyer representatives. Such distinctions highlight an agent's professionalism.

Codes of Ethics

Professional associations promote ethics through published codes of conduct their members commit to upholding. These codes cover brokerages and agents.

The National Association of REALTORS'® Code of Ethics is the industry's best-known, covering duty, loyalty, disclosure, cooperation, and more. Members also pledge to abide by Standards of Practice and Statements of Professionalism, elaborating on the Code's principles. State and local associations of REALTORS® adopt this Code as their model.

Beyond REALTORS®, most states base their real estate licensee codes of conduct on a model code drafted by the National Association of Real Estate License Law Officials (NARELLO). This model code addresses similar duties and practices. Adhering to these codes fosters ethical rigor.

Core Principles

Certain core principles form real estate ethics' cornerstones regardless of any single group's code. Truth, honesty, integrity, accountability, and loyalty universally define ethical practice.

Agents exhibit truthfulness by transparently conveying factual information free of deception. They demonstrate honesty through sincerity in recommendations and counsel. Integrity manifests in incorruptible adherence to values despite temptations. Accepting consequences for actions and failures reflects accountability. Prioritizing clients' interests above self-benefit shows loyalty.

These fundamental virtues inform the judgment of ethical practitioners. They steer professionals away from misguided motives like greed or concealment and towards client-centered service.

Typical Dilemmas

While ideals seem clear, real estate professionals inevitably encounter tricky situations testing their ethical mettle. Recognizing common dilemmas prepares agents to react with principle.

Confidentiality concerns pose dilemmas, as when a seller requests agents conceal known defects from buyers. So do situations pitting self-interest against duty, like advising on a lower offer that secures quicker commissions. The dual agency produces divided loyalties. Bidding wars and tight markets also tempt agents away from transparency.

But preparation creates a readiness to meet challenges with virtue. Having the courage to make ethical choices despite surrounding pressures or incentives defines credible professionals.

Ethical Decision-Making

Logical frameworks support an agent's ability to methodically resolve ethical dilemmas as they arise. These decision-making models provide helpful guidance.

A common approach involves first gathering information to clearly understand involved interests and implications. With clearer situational awareness, reflecting on how core principles apply to the circumstances and weighing potential actions against them allows for more aligned choices.

Consulting codes of ethics, regulatory guidelines, peer perspectives, and professional mentors can further illuminate suitable solutions. Taking time for conscious deliberation leads to ethically sound outcomes.

Professional Best Practices

Day-to-day real estate business operations present countless opportunities to implement ethical best practices. Small choices fostering integrity and accountability have an impact.

Respecting agency relationships shows integrity. So does proactively disclosing material facts to clients, even unpleasant realities they may not want to hear. Strictly separating fiduciary obligations and any personal interests prevents conflicts. Extending honest, unbiased counsel without regard for the impact of transactions on commissions demonstrates accountability.

Agents hoping to excel as consummate professionals let principles, not transactions or gain, motivate their actions. Consistent ethical conduct builds rewarding careers.

Risk Management

In such a complex, high-stakes industry, real estate professionals consistently face risks requiring prudent management. To limit legal exposures and operational vulnerabilities, practitioners employ diverse risk mitigation strategies. This section explores techniques from insurance to documentation that provide critical protections for agents and brokerages. Gaining competency in risk analysis and reduction safeguards careers and enables confident navigation of the inevitable uncertainties of deals.

Documentation

Meticulous transaction documentation provides one of the strongest foundations for risk management. Written records help prevent misunderstandings while memorializing key information.

Real estate professionals should document everything of significance, including listing terms, property conditions, client instructions, disclosed facts, agreements, and other substantial communications. Detailed records evidence the full circumstances surrounding transactions.

Digital organization systems help properly retain key documents. Paper trails become invaluable if disputes arise regarding past transactions. Therefore, diligence with documentation offers enduring risk protection.

Disclosure

Upfront disclosure of material facts similarly constitutes a prudent risk management tactic. Real estate agents carry legal duties of honesty and transparency. Failure to disclose known issues exposes agents to risks.

If problems surface that were not disclosed to buyers, they may allege misrepresentation and threaten lawsuits. However, relaying adverse facts about properties or transactions promptly after discovery helps agents demonstrate good faith. It shows clients were fully informed, preventing cover-up accusations.

While disclosing may displease clients, forthright transparency ultimately protects them and mitigates an agent's liability risks. It evidences responsible representation.

Agreements in Writing

Committing all agreements with clients to writing provides another means for managing deal risks. Oral agreements invite misunderstandings and problems with enforceability, but writings clarify expectations.

Listing agreements, buyer/tenant representation contracts, amendments, and any other collaborations should be memorialized in official documents outlining terms. E-signatures make documentation convenient.

Consulting legal counsel when crafting customized agreements also helps identify areas of concern. Written records prevent confused recollections and contract disputes. They cement mutual understanding.

Insurance Coverage

Maintaining adequate insurance coverage allows real estate professionals to defray potential liability risks. Policies cover expenses stemming from various legal actions clients could take in the event of agent errors or omissions.

Standard policies include errors and omissions (E&O) insurance protecting against alleged misconduct and professional liability insurance covering negligent guidance. Broader umbrella policies offer added peace of mind for larger brokerages.

Reviewing risks, assets, locations, and business structures with qualified insurance advisors ensures optimal coverage. Proper policies make damages stemming from unforeseen circumstances more manageable.

MLS Listing Review

Double-checking Multiple Listing Service (MLS) listings and property data helps agents catch mistakes before they propagate and cause problems. Relying solely on others for accuracy, invites trouble.

Reviewing listings for errors regarding property details, boundaries, bedroom/bath counts, amenities, HOAs, zoning, etc., limits misinformation. Verifying required disclosures helps as well. Also, scrutinizing listing remarks for appropriate, lawful language is wise.

While MLS input largely falls to assistants, accountability rests with agents. Thus, developing quality assurance processes to validate details breeds stability. Preventing issues is more effective than correcting them.

Transaction Oversight

Diligent transaction oversight provides vital risk control, enabling agents to monitor a deal's progress and intercede at signs of trouble. Waiting idly is never a good idea.

Examples of oversight include closely tracking critical dates, following up on required tasks, ensuring client compliance, monitoring loan processes, validating closing figures, and reviewing documentation thoroughly. Proactive engagement mitigates surprises.

Utilizing checklists and reminders facilitates organized oversight. Sharp transaction management means recognizing risks before they become crises. Agents who stay on top of transactions limit their vulnerability.

Chapter 8: State-Specific Regulations and Practices

Real estate regulations, licensing requirements, commissions, and contractual rules can vary significantly from state to state. In this chapter, we will take a deeper look at the unique real estate laws and practices in 10 major states: California, Florida, Texas, New York, Illinois, Georgia, Arizona, North Carolina, Colorado, and Washington.

California

The California Department of Real Estate (DRE) oversees real estate licensing and regulations in the state. To become a salesperson in California, you must complete 3 college-level real estate courses totaling at least 99 hours and then pass the California Real Estate Salesperson Exam. To become a broker, you must have 2 years of full-time salesperson experience in the last 5 years, complete 8 college-level courses totaling at least 168 hours, and pass the California Real Estate Broker Exam. Continuing education is required for the renewal of both salesperson and broker licenses.

The California Association of Realtors (C.A.R.) is the state's largest trade association, providing forms, professional development, advocacy, and other services to over 200,000 members. C.A.R. has also created the California Regional Multiple Listing Service (CRMLS) to consolidate MLS databases across the state.

Key elements of California real estate contracts include:

- Disclosure forms - sellers must disclose any known defects, hazards, or facts that may affect value.
- Contingencies - common contingencies concern financing, appraisal, inspections, and sale of the buyer's current home.
- Date of possession - details when the buyer takes ownership and gains access to the property.
- Agency relationships - outlines the agency duties between agent, buyer, and seller.
- Mediation provision - requires mediation before lawsuits in the event of a dispute.

Florida

The Florida Real Estate Commission, within the Florida Department of Business and Professional Regulation, oversees real estate licensing and regulations in Florida. To become licensed as a sales associate, you must be at least 18 years old, complete 63 hours of pre-licensing education, and pass the state exam. To become a broker, you must have a high school diploma or equivalent, hold an active sales associate license, complete 72 hours of pre-licensing education, and pass the state broker exam. Continuing education is required for both licenses.

The Florida Realtors Association provides political advocacy, professional development, networking opportunities, standard forms, and more to over 150,000 members across the state. The Florida Realtors operates Florida Realtors Information Systems (FRIS) and Sunny MLS as statewide MLS databases.

Key elements of Florida real estate contracts include:

- Seller's Property Disclosure - requires sellers to disclose any known defects to prospective buyers.
- Inspection clause - allows the buyer a specified number of days to have the property inspected.
- Appraisal contingency - makes the sale conditional upon the property appraising for not less than the sale price.
- Radon gas testing - gives the buyer the right to test for radon gas.
- Financing contingency - makes the sale contingent on the buyer obtaining financing.
- Risk of loss provision - states which party bears the risk if property damage occurs before closing.

Texas

The Texas Real Estate Commission administers licensure and regulations for real estate professionals in Texas. To become a sales agent, you must complete 6 hours of core real estate courses plus 54 hours of electives, then pass the Texas Real Estate Salesperson Exam. To become a broker, you must have been a sales agent for 4 years during the past 6 years, complete 6 core course hours plus 54 elective hours, and pass the Texas Real Estate Broker Exam. Every 2 years, agents must also complete 18 hours of continuing education.

The Texas Association of Realtors has over 140,000 members and provides professional development programs, advocacy, standard forms, and more. The Texas Real Estate Information Systems, Inc. (TREIS) operates the TREIS MLS to consolidate property listing data across the state.

Key elements of Texas real estate contracts include:

- Seller Disclosure Notice - requires the seller to disclose all known defects or other important information about the property.
- Option Fee - this is an optional fee paid by a prospective buyer to take a property off the market for a set period of time.
- Loan Assumption - states the rules if a buyer wants to assume the seller's existing mortgage loan.
- Sale of Other Property Contingency - makes the transaction contingent on the sale of the buyer's current home.
- Title Policy - the title company agrees to provide a specified policy to the buyer.

- Earnest Money - The buyer submits an earnest money deposit, which is credited at closing.

New York

The New York Department of State's Division of Licensing Services oversees real estate licensing and regulations in New York. To qualify for a salesperson license, you must complete 75 hours of approved pre-licensing education plus pass a state exam. To become an associate broker, you must have 2 years of licensed salesperson experience and complete 150 additional education hours. For broker licenses, you must have substantial experience as a salesperson or associate broker plus complete qualifying education. License renewal requires continuing education.

The New York State Association of Realtors provides advocacy, networking, standard forms, MLS services, and professional development opportunities to over 60,000 members. The New York State MLS (MLSLI), owned by the Long Island Board of Realtors, serves over 35,000 subscribers statewide.

Key elements of New York real estate purchase contracts include:

- Property Condition Disclosure Statement - requires the seller to disclose any known defects.
- Mortgage Contingency Clause - makes the contract contingent on the buyer obtaining financing.
- Attorney Review Clause - gives the attorneys for both parties the right to cancel the contract.
- Rider - used to add special terms, conditions, or contingencies to the contract.
- Holdover Tenant Clause - details procedures if a tenant remains on the property after closing.
- Lead Paint Disclosure - informs buyers of potential hazards related to lead-based paint.

Illinois

The Illinois Department of Financial and Professional Regulation licenses and regulates real estate professionals in Illinois. To become a managing broker or leasing agent, you must have a high school diploma, complete a 45-hour broker pre-license course, and pass a state licensing exam. A managing broker can then sponsor other brokers and salespeople. Salespersons must be sponsored by a managing broker. Continuing education is required for license renewal.

The Illinois Realtors Association promotes professional standards, lobbies for its over 50,000 members, and provides education programs and networking opportunities across the state. The Midwest Real Estate Data LLC (MRED) MLS covers over 45,000 real estate professionals in northern Illinois.

Key components of Illinois real estate sale contracts include:

- Residential Real Property Disclosure Report - sellers must disclose all known material defects.
- Attorney Review Period - attorneys have 5 days to review the contract.

- Home Inspection Contingency Clause - makes the sale contingent on a professional inspection.
  - Appraisal Contingency - sale depends on the property appraising for the purchase price.
  - Affidavit of Title - seller affidavits regarding transferability of title.
  - Survey - The buyer has the right to obtain an official survey of the property.
  - Earnest Money - The buyer submits an earnest money deposit, which is credited at closing.

Georgia

The Georgia Real Estate Commission regulates licensure and real estate practices in Georgia. To become a licensed real estate salesperson, you must be at least 18 years old, complete a 75-hour salesperson pre-license course, and pass the state exam. To get a broker license, you must have at least 3 years of salesperson experience, complete a 50-hour broker pre-license course, and pass the state broker exam. Continuing education is required for license renewal.

The Georgia Association of Realtors promotes the interests of its 60,000+ members by providing professional development, networking events, advocacy, standardized forms, and MLS services. The Georgia MLS covers over 65,000 subscribers statewide.

Key components of Georgia real estate sales contracts include:

- Seller's Property Disclosure Statement - requires sellers to disclose all known defects and issues.
- Right of Entry provision - allows the buyer and agents to access the property for inspections.
- Financing Contingency Clause - makes the contract contingent on the buyer getting suitable financing.
- Wood Infestation Report - gives the buyer the right to obtain a termite inspection.
- Loan Assumption Clause - sets terms for the buyer to assume the seller's mortgage.
- Earnest Money - The buyer submits a good faith deposit that is credited at closing.

Arizona

The Arizona Department of Real Estate (ADRE) oversees licensing and regulation of real estate professionals in Arizona. To become a salesperson, you must complete 90 hours of pre-licensing education and then pass the state exam. For a broker's license, you must document 2 years of salesperson experience in the last 5 years, take 90 hours of broker pre-license courses, and pass the broker exam. Ongoing continuing education is required for license renewal.

The Arizona Association of Realtors promotes ethics, advocacy, MLS services, and the interests of over 45,000 members across the state. The statewide Arizona Regional MLS (ARMLS) covers over 45,000 real estate professionals.

Key elements of Arizona real estate purchase contracts include:

- Seller's Property Disclosure Statement (SPDS) - requires the seller to disclose all known material facts about the property's condition.
- Inspection Addendum - allows time for the buyer to complete a professional property inspection after the offer is accepted.
- Loan Assumption Addendum - sets terms for the buyer to assume the seller's existing mortgage.
- "As Is" Provision - agrees to purchase the property in the condition it currently is without requiring repairs.
- Title Insurance provision - requires title insurance to protect the buyer.
- Close of Escrow Clause - sets the closing date when the transaction will become final.

North Carolina

The North Carolina Real Estate Commission regulates licensure and real estate practices in North Carolina. To get a real estate salesperson license, you must complete a 75-hour pre-licensing course and pass the state exam. For a broker license, you must document 2 years of full-time salesperson experience or 4 years of part-time experience, complete a 45-hour broker pre-licensing course, and pass the state exam. Continuing education is required for license renewal every 2 years.

The North Carolina Association of Realtors promotes high professional standards and the interests of its 45,000+ members through advocacy, education programs, networking events, and standardized forms. The Information Network of North Carolina (IANN) provides statewide MLS services to over 20,000 subscribers.

Key elements of North Carolina real estate contracts include:

- Disclosure Statement - requires the seller to disclose all known issues and material facts about the property.
- Due Diligence Fees - fees paid by the buyer to research zoning, permits, environmental issues, etc.
- Loan Assumption Clause - sets terms for the buyer to take over the seller's existing mortgage.
- Home Inspection Contingency - makes the contract contingent on a professional home inspection that is satisfactory.
- Lead-Based Paint or Lead-Based Paint Hazard Addendum - discloses risks related to lead-based paint.
- Mediation Provision - requires mediation to resolve disputes before a lawsuit may be filed.

Colorado

The Colorado Division of Real Estate regulates licensure and real estate practices in Colorado. To become a real estate broker, you must complete a minimum of 168 hours of real estate courses plus 24 hours of broker courses, document 2 years of experience, and pass the state broker exam. To get a salesperson license, you must work under a licensed Colorado broker, complete a minimum of 168 hours of real estate courses, and pass the salesperson exam. Ongoing continuing education is required.

The Colorado Association of Realtors promotes ethics and advocates for over 25,000 members. The statewide REcolorado MLS includes listings from over 25,000 real estate professionals.

Key components of Colorado real estate contracts include:

- Seller's Property Disclosure - requires the seller to disclose all known material facts about the property's condition.
- Inspection Objection Deadline - the date by which the buyer must object to inspection results.
- Title Insurance Clause - requires title insurance to protect the buyer.
- Survey Provision - gives the buyer the option to have the property surveyed.
- Mineral Rights Addendum - details ownership rights of subsurface minerals.
- HOA/Condo Addendum - addresses obligations for HOA or condo association fees and disclosures.
- Water Rights Addendum - states ownership rights for water sources on the property.

Washington

The Washington State Department of Licensing regulates real estate professionals in Washington. To become a managing broker, you must document 3 years of licensed experience, complete 90 hours of brokerage management courses, and pass the state exam. To get a broker license, you must complete a 60-hour pre-license course and pass the exam. For salesperson licenses, you must complete a 60-hour pre-license course. First renewals require 30 hours of continuing education. The Washington Realtors Association promotes professional standards and advocacy for its 25,000+ members across the state. Northwest MLS provides MLS services to over 30,000 real estate brokers and agents in Washington.

Key elements of Washington real estate purchase and sale agreements include:

- Seller Disclosure Statement - requires the seller to disclose all known material facts about the property.
- Inspection Contingency Clause - gives the buyer time to have inspections completed after mutual acceptance.
- Appraisal Contingency - ensures the appraised value meets the sale price.
- Title Insurance Clause - requires title insurance to protect the buyer's interests.
- Lead-Based Paint Pamphlet - provides information on risks related to lead-based paint.
- Closing Costs Section - outlines which costs are paid by buyer vs. seller.
- Earnest Money Receipt - acknowledges buyer's good faith deposit amount.

Section II: Practical Preparation

Chapter 9: Study Strategies and Tips

Passing the real estate salesperson licensing exam requires dedication, focus, and strategic preparation. With so much material to cover, from local regulations to math calculations, having an effective study plan is critical. This chapter provides you with techniques and tips to make the most of your study time. By implementing targeted strategies for note-taking, memory retention, and time management, you can assimilate the breadth of information in an organized, productive manner.

Whether just starting their preparation or looking to optimize their efforts, the guidance in this chapter empowers you to study smart. With concrete examples and actionable advice, it transforms the exam from an obstacle into an achievable goal. Now, let's explore specific techniques to enact this meaningful journey.

Effective Note-Taking

Effective note-taking is crucial for successful studying, especially when preparing for a licensing exam. Begin by maintaining a clean and organized study notebook dedicated to exam-related notes. Use tabbed dividers to separate sections like "Laws & Regulations" or "Math Formulas," and develop a consistent page numbering system for easy reference. Print digital materials and insert them into the relevant sections.

Start each new content area with an overview page summarizing key themes and topics. As you progress, continually add to this overview to create clear connections between details. Use bullet points within each section to neatly summarize key takeaways, maintaining topical continuity. Avoid lengthy paragraphs and leave space between bullets for additional thoughts.

For visual learners, enhance your notes with concept maps, charts, and diagrams that illustrate connections between topics. Studies suggest that incorporating images improves information retention. Annotate printed materials by highlighting main ideas, using different colors for various types of information, and writing brief clarifying notes in the margins. Be selective with highlighting, focusing on truly significant points.

Memory Techniques

To remember information effectively, you can use memory techniques that make the material stick in your mind. One method is using mnemonic devices, which associate information with something memorable. Acronyms, like "PEMDAS" for the order of operations in math, and acrostics, such as creating a phrase with the first letter of each word matching the items to remember, are helpful. Chunking involves breaking long strings of information into smaller, more manageable parts. Rhyming can also aid recall, connecting concepts in a memorable way.

Visualization is another powerful technique. Create vivid mental images related to the information you want to remember. For example, visualize a property's square footage multiplied by the price per square foot. Add color, texture, emotions, movement, and spatial arrangements to intensify these mental images. Repetition, reading key points aloud, and rewriting important information strengthen memory pathways. Relate new information to what you already know, connecting processes or vocabulary to familiar examples. Finally, teaching concepts to others helps reinforce your own understanding by explaining and framing the information in ways that resonate.

Time Management Tips

Managing your time well is important, especially when you have exams, work, family, and other responsibilities. To do this, create a routine that helps you make the most of your study time. Break down your study goals into smaller, achievable tasks for each day and week leading up to the exam. For example, plan to cover a certain number of pages each day and take a (part of a) practice test every Saturday. This way, your preparation becomes more manageable, and you can track your progress.

Focus on the areas that you find most challenging. Identify your weaknesses by assessing your performance on practice tests. Make a list of the topics that you struggle with the most and prioritize studying them during your peak mental energy times. Instead of cramming large amounts of material at the last minute, aim for steady and consistent studying over time. Understand the material rather than just memorizing it, as this leads to better retention. Also, choose optimal times for studying when you feel most alert and focused, and create a distraction-free environment to maximize your concentration. Practice taking timed tests to improve your time management skills and boost your exam scores.

Chapter 10: Practice Scenarios

After covering the theoretical knowledge required to pass the real estate salesperson licensing exam in previous chapters, this chapter focuses on providing you with opportunities to apply that knowledge through real-world simulations. Role-playing exercises, mock negotiations, and valuation exercises will enable you to put their learning into practice in low-stakes environments. Gaining hands-on experience with common scenarios agents face will ensure you are fully prepared not just for the exam but for the daily realities of life as a real estate professional.

Role-Playing - Agent-Client Interactions

Navigating agent-client relationships is a foundational skill in real estate. Effective communication and the ability to manage clients' expectations are key to success. The following role-playing scenarios provide you with a chance to simulate common interactions with both buyers and sellers. Practicing these conversations will develop the soft skills crucial to thriving in real estate.

First Meeting with New Buyer

Agent: Hi Susan, I'm so glad we could meet today to discuss your home-buying goals. As your agent, I'm committed to guiding you through this process and helping you find the perfect home. To start, what price range are you hoping to stay within? What areas are you interested in? How many bedrooms and bathrooms are you looking for?

Client: Hi! I'm hoping to keep it under $300,000. I'm open to different neighborhoods but want good schools. Ideally, 4 bedrooms, 2-3 bathrooms, with a big backyard.

Agent: Great, that gives me a good sense of your must-haves. Let's pull up the MLS and look at some options that meet those needs. I'd also like to get pre-approved with a lender so we know your price ceiling...

Following Up with Unhappy Buyer

Agent: Hi, Matt. I know you were disappointed we lost that bidding war on Elm Street last week. I'm so sorry we couldn't make that work. How are you feeling about moving forward with the search?

Client: Pretty frustrated, to be honest. That house seemed perfect, but we just can't compete with these cash offers over asking. Feels like we'll never find the right place at this rate.

Agent: I know how disheartening it can feel to miss out on a place you love. But I want you to know I'm still committed to finding your dream home. Let's expand the search a bit into nearby neighborhoods - there are some great options popping up. We'll make sure to craft competitive offers and get your offer accepted soon!

First Meeting with New Seller

Agent: Sarah, thank you for meeting with me today to discuss selling your home. Tell me a bit more about your goals and motivations around selling at this time.

Client: Well, we need more space now that we have two kids. And prices seem to be up in this neighborhood, so I'm hoping to take advantage of that. We need to move within 3 months for my husband's job transfer.

Agent: Perfect, that timeline works well with getting your home prepped for sale. Let me walk through, and we can discuss first impressions, presentation, and pricing strategy to get this sold quickly and for top dollar. I know the local market really well, so lean on my expertise...

Presenting an Offer to a Seller

Agent: Hi Cindy. We received an offer this morning that I'd like to go over with you. They offered $485,000 with an escalation clause of up to $500,000. They've asked for closing costs of 3%. There's a home inspection contingency and $5000 in earnest money. What are your initial thoughts?

Client: Hmm, lower than our asking price, but the escalation helps. I'm okay covering some closing costs. The inspection request seems fair. I'm a bit concerned about appraisal issues. What's your advice on countering or accepting as is?

Agent: Great questions. In my professional opinion, this is a strong offer given current market conditions. I advise accepting the escalation clause, countering at 1% closing costs, and sticking firm on price. Let me walk you through my recommendations in detail...

Handling Objections from a Buyer

Client: The kitchen is pretty small and dated. And the carpets look worn. I don't know that this house is worth what they're asking.

Agent: I understand your concerns. While it could use some cosmetic upgrades, this home is priced really competitively for the neighborhood and meets your key criteria. Making some small renovations down the line could truly make it your dream home. And we may be able to negotiate appliances or closing credits. Let's dig deeper on the pros here...

Presenting a Market Analysis to a Seller

Agent: Based on the comps I pulled, homes in this area have been selling in the $450K-$475K range, given the market conditions. With some strategic pricing and marketing, I think we could reasonably list for $465K. This balances maximizing value with attracting buyers through more affordability. What are your thoughts on this recommended list price?

Client: Honestly, I was hoping for a $500K minimum. We put a lot into the kitchen remodel and landscaping. I think this home shows much better than the comps. Can we start on the higher end with room to negotiate down?

Agent: I understand wanting to maximize the sale price. Let's look again at the data and recent sales and determine where there might be room to inch up closer to your goal.

Mock Contract Negotiations

Buyer's Agent: Thank you for taking the time to discuss the inspection report findings. As you know, the inspection uncovered foundation cracks, a roof leak, and a faulty HVAC system. We'd like to request repairs in those three areas before closing.

Seller's Agent: I reviewed the inspection with my clients. They are willing to repair the roof and HVAC but feel the foundation cracks are a pre-existing condition they cannot take responsibility for.

Buyer's Agent: We understand your clients' position, but we must address the foundation concerns before moving forward. Would your clients consider a credit of $5,000 to go towards a structural engineer assessment and future repairs?

Seller's Agent: I can take that back to them, but I doubt they will agree to an open-ended credit. The most they may be able to do is a $2,500 credit for the assessment alone.

Buyer's Agent: We are flexible on the credit amount but need assurance the issue will be evaluated by a structural engineer. Would your sellers agree to a $3,000 credit for the assessment and an additional provision that we can renegotiate repairs based on the engineer's recommendations?

Seller's Agent: Let me present that offer. I think we may be able to make this work with a $3,000 assessment credit and a clause to renegotiate specific repairs after getting the engineer's report. I'll be in touch soon.

Buyer's Agent: Sounds good; please let me know once you've spoken with them. I'm hopeful we can come to an agreement that satisfies both parties.

Property Valuation Exercises

Comparative Market Analysis

- Provide the property details: 3 bedroom, 2 bathroom single family home, 1,800 square feet, finished basement, 2-car garage, half acre lot
    - Provide recent comparable sales in the same neighborhood:
        - House A: 3 bed, 2 bath, 1,750 sq ft, no basement, 2-car garage, 0.4-acre lot - Sold for $275,000
        - House B: 4 bed, 2.5 bath, 2,000 sq ft, partially finished basement, 2-car garage, 0.35-acre lot - Sold for $290,000
        - House C: 3 bed, 1.5 bath, 1,600 sq ft, no basement, 1-car garage, 0.5-acre lot - Sold for $260,000
    - Determine a list price range using the comparable sales data

Solution:

House A sold for $275,000

House B sold for $290,000

House C sold for $260,000

The subject property is most similar to House A in size and features. Adjusting for the partially finished basement, it would likely sell for slightly more than House A.

Suggested List Price Range: $280,000 - $285,000

Price Per Square Foot Calculation

- Provide property details: 2,500 square foot home on a 15,000 square foot lot
- Calculate the price per square foot if the home is listed at:
  - $500,000
  - $475,000
  - $450,000

Solution:

2,500 sq ft home on 15,000 sq ft lot

If listed at:

$500,000, the price per square foot is $500,000 / 2,500 sq ft = $200/sq ft

$475,000, the price per square foot is $475,000 / 2,500 sq ft = $190/sq ft

$450,000, the price per square foot is $450,000 / 2,500 sq ft = $180/sq ft

Gross Rent Multiplier

- Provide property details: Duplex with 2 bedroom, 1 bathroom units renting for $1,000/month each
- Provide average GRM for the area: 8
- Calculate the estimated value of the duplex using the GRM

Solution:

Duplex with 2 units renting for $1,000/month each

Market GRM is 8

Monthly Rent = $1,000 x 2 = $2,000

Annual Rent = $2,000 x 12 = $24,000

Estimated Value = Annual Rent x GRM = $24,000 x 8 = $192,000

Capitalization Rate Calculation

- Provide property details: 4-unit apartment building generating $60,000 in annual gross rental income
- Provide operating expenses of $15,000/year
- Calculate the capitalization rate if the property sells for $600,000

Solution:

4-unit apartment building with $60,000 gross annual rent

$15,000 in annual operating expenses

Sold for $600,000

Net Operating Income = Gross Annual Rent - Operating Expenses = $60,000 - $15,000 = $45,000

Capitalization Rate = Net Operating Income / Sale Price = $45,000 / $600,000 = 0.075 or 7.5%

Chapter 11: Review Quizzes

Reviewing key concepts through quizzes is an essential part of exam preparation. This chapter provides quizzes covering all the major topics in real estate licensing to help reinforce your knowledge and identify any weak areas that may need further study. With a combination of fact-based and application questions, these quizzes will build both your understanding and test-taking skills. Use them as a self-assessment tool to track your progress as you work through the book.

Quiz 1: Property Ownership and Land Use

Q1.   Which of the following most accurately describes the bundle of rights associated with property ownership?
   A.   The right of possession, the right of control, and the right of exclusion
   B.   The right of liability, the right of transferability, and the right of enjoyment
   C.   The right of destruction, the right of nonconformity, and the right of disposition
   D.   The right of encumbrance, the right of easement, and the right of accession

Q2.   What term describes the legal process in which the government takes private property for public use while providing just compensation to the owner?
   A.   Promulgation
   B.   Escheatment
   C.   Eminent domain
   D.   Encumbrance

Q3.   Which of the following statements accurately describes a life estate?
   A.   A form of ownership held only for the life of the owner
   B.   A fractional ownership share in a property
   C.   A non-possessory interest in land
   D.   An ownership interest held in perpetuity

Q4.   What is the difference between a license and an easement?
   A.   A license is written, while an easement is oral
   B.   A license can be revoked, while an easement cannot
   C.   A license requires a deed, while an easement does not
   D.   A license requires recording, while an easement does not

Q5.   Which of the following is true of alienation clauses?

A.   They require all transfers of ownership to be approved by the HOA

B.   They prohibit restrictions on selling or transferring property

C.   They are unenforceable under federal law

D.   They require the seller to offer their property to the HOA first

Q6.   Which type of property ownership only applies in some states?

A.   Tenancy in common

B.   Sole ownership

C.   Join tenancy

D.   Community property

Q7.   What is the difference between adverse possession and prescriptive easement?

A.   Adverse possession can lead to ownership, while prescriptive easements only lead to use rights

B.   Prescriptive easements require payment, while adverse possession does not

C.   Adverse possession applies to land, while prescriptive easements apply to use

D.   Prescriptive easements require court action, while adverse possession does not

Q8.   Which of the following is needed to successfully claim adverse possession?

A.   Exclusive, open, and notorious use

B.   Continuous, hostile, and notorious use

C.   Notorious, uninterrupted, and stealthy use

D.   Open, limited, and uncontested use

Q9.   What is the difference between an assessor's plat and a record of the survey?

A.   Assessor's plans define parcel boundaries while records of survey locate improvements

B.   Records of survey define boundaries while the assessor's plans locate improvements

C.   Assessor's plats define easements while records of survey define parcel boundaries

D.   Records of survey locate easements while assessor's plats define parcel boundaries

Q10.   Which action below meets the open and notorious requirement for adverse possession?

    A.   Putting up a fence around the disputed land

    B.   Using the land while trying to hide the use

    C.   Occasionally walking across the disputed land

    D.   Secretly building a structure on the land

Q11.   What is the purpose of governmental police power?

    A.   To generate tax revenue from property owners

    B.   To take privately owned land for public benefit

    C.   To regulate the use of land in the interest of public welfare

    D.   To ensure health and safety through the court system

Q12.   Which of the following is considered an encumbrance on real property?

    A.   Revocable license

    B.   Utility easement

    C.   Special assessment

    D.   Voluntary lien

Q13.   What is the difference between tangible and intangible personal property?

    A.   Tangible property has a physical form, while intangible does not

    B.   Tangible property includes real estate, while intangible does not

    C.   Tangible property excludes intellectual creations, while intangible does not

    D.   Tangible property cannot be destroyed, while intangible can

Q14.   Which of the following types of ownership MUST be created by a written document?

    A.   Joint tenancy

    B.   Tenancy in common

    C.   Tenancy by the entirety

    D.   Community property

Q15.   What is the definition of constructive notice?

   A.   Notice given verbally about encumbrances

   B.   Notice published in local newspapers

   C.   Notice inferred from properly recorded documents

   D.   Direct notice sent to affected parties

Q16.   Which of the following statements is true of the public trust doctrine?

   A.   It prohibits all private use of navigable waterways

   B.   It conveys ownership of submerged lands to the government

   C.   It regulates the use of non-navigable waterways

   D.   It transfers beach property to public ownership

Q17.   What is the difference between an affirmative easement and a negative easement?

   A.   Affirmative easements benefit the property, while negative easements burden the property

   B.   Negative easements are written, while affirmative easements are oral

   C.   Affirmative easements are revocable, while negative easements are not

   D.   Negative easements require compensation, while affirmative easements do not

Q18.   Which of the following types of ownership includes the right of survivorship?

   A.   Tenants in common

   B.   Joint tenancy

   C.   Tenancy by the entirety

   D.   Community property

Q19.   What is the difference between a permit and a variance?

   A.   Permits authorize desired uses while variances waive zoning requirements

   B.   Variances are allowed uses while permits waive zoning rules

   C.   Permits are issued by courts, while variances are issued by zoning boards

   D.   Variances authorize future uses, while permits allow existing uses to continue

Q20. What type of zoning covers a group of two or more buildings with different heights, setbacks, or other site characteristics?

    A. Form-based zoning

    B. Incentive zoning

    C. Mixed-use zoning

    D. Planned unit development

Q21. What is the definition of condemnation as it relates to eminent domain?

    A. The process of removing tenants after property acquisition

    B. The dispute resolution process when the compensation amount is challenged

    C. The initial notification given to property owners about the taking

    D. The legal proceeding to acquire private property for public use

Q22. Which of the following is true about novel estates?

    A. They are interests in real property that endure for a fixed period.

    B. They are newly created real property interests by an owner.

    C. They are ownership interests that can be inherited only by immediate family.

    D. They are new forms of ownership prohibited by common law.

Q23. A landowner grants part of their property to a local utility company to install electrical equipment that services the surrounding area. What type of easement has been created?

    A. An affirmative easement

    B. A negative easement

    C. An appurtenant easement

    D. An easement in gross

Q24. Which of the following statements is true regarding encroachments?

    A. They only involve man-made structures extending into another's property.

    B. They must be permitted by the affected owner to be legally valid.

    C. They do not confer any property rights to the encroaching party.

    D. They can potentially lead to adverse possession claims.

Q25.   Which of the following is required to create an enforceable land use restriction?

A.   Consideration and appurtenance of the land

B.   Recordation and mutual assent

C.   Signature of all impacted owners

D.   Approval by a zoning commission

Quiz 1 Answer Key

1) Answer: A

Explanation: The bundle of rights associated with property ownership includes the right of possession (occupy/use property), the right of control (determine how it's used), and the right of exclusion (determine who uses it).

2) Answer: C

Explanation: Eminent domain is the right of the government to take private property for public use while providing just compensation to the owner. It does not include the right to take property for private use.

3) Answer: A

Explanation: A life estate is a form of ownership interest in real property that ends upon the death of the owner. It allows the owner to possess, use, and obtain profits from the property during their lifetime.

4) Answer: B

Explanation: A license is revocable at will, while an easement is an irrevocable right attached to the land. An easement holder has an interest in the property, while a license holder does not.

5) Answer: D

Explanation: Alienation clauses require sellers to first offer their property for sale to the HOA before selling to the general public. They do NOT prohibit transfers or require HOA approval.

6) Answer: D

Explanation: The others are all common forms of ownership, but not all states have principles of community property.

7) Answer: C

Explanation: Adverse possession can potentially lead to legal ownership if all requirements are met. Prescriptive easements only lead to use rights, not ownership.

8) Answer: B

Explanation: The elements of adverse possession are continuous, hostile, open, notorious, exclusive, and uninterrupted use for the statutory period.

9) Answer: D

Explanation: Assessor's plats are used specifically to define parcel boundaries for tax purposes. Records of the survey identify the location of improvements and easements.

10) Answer: A

Explanation: Open and notorious use requires the adverse possessor to use the land such that the legal owner is put on notice. Using the land openly, such as by building a fence, satisfies this requirement.

11)   Answer: C

Explanation: Police power allows the government to regulate private land use to promote public health, safety, morals, and general welfare. It does NOT involve takings or generating revenue.

12)   Answer: C

Explanation: An encumbrance is a right or interest in land that diminishes its value to the landowner. A special assessment is considered an encumbrance because it must be paid off when the property is sold.

13)   Answer: A

Explanation: Tangible personal property has a physical form, while intangible personal property does not. Intangible property includes things like copyrights, patents, and trademarks.

14)   Answer: C

Explanation: Tenancy by the entirety must be expressly created by a written document and meet specific requirements. The other types can be created by deeds, actions, or default rules.

15)   Answer: C

Explanation: Constructive notice occurs when buyers are assumed to know about encumbrances and other matters because they are properly recorded in public land records.

16)   Answer: B

Explanation: The public trust doctrine holds that submerged lands under navigable waters are held in trust by the state for the public, while private use is not necessarily prohibited.

17)   Answer: A

Explanation: An affirmative easement grants the easement holder the right to use the burdened property in some way. A negative easement limits the owner of the burdened property from doing something.

18)   Answer: B

Explanation: Joint tenancy includes the right of survivorship, meaning that if one owner dies, their interest passes to the surviving owner(s). Tenants in common and community property do not have rights of survivorship.

19)   Answer: A

Explanation: Permits authorize land uses that are allowed under current zoning. Variances waive zoning requirements to allow non-permitted uses.

20)   Answer: D

Explanation: Planned unit developments allow custom zoning standards to accommodate developments with a variety of building types, heights, or arrangements.

21)   Answer: D

Explanation: Condemnation is the legal proceeding used by the government to acquire private property under eminent domain. It leads to a court judgment transferring title.

22)   Answer: B

Explanation: Novel estates are interests in real property intentionally created and defined by the existing owner, as distinguished from standard recognized estates.

23)   Answer: D

Explanation: An easement in gross benefits the holder independently of any land owned. Utility easements are typically easements in gross since they benefit the utility company directly.

24)   Answer: D

Explanation: Encroachments involve improvements physically extending into another's land. They can provide the basis for adverse possession if not addressed promptly.

25)   Answer: B

Explanation: Enforceable land use restrictions must be consensual, in writing, recorded, and appurtenant to the land. Consideration is not a legal requirement.

Quiz 2: Real Estate Law

Q1. A property owner executes a general warranty deed for the sale of their property. What protection does this give the buyer?

    A.   It guarantees the property is free of encumbrances

    B.   It promises the seller has a simple title

    C.   It provides title insurance for the buyer

    D.   It warrants the property condition is as promised

Q2. Which essential element is needed to create an enforceable contract?

    A.   Equitable remedies

    B.   Adequate consideration

    C.   Notarized signatures

    D.   Competent parties

Q3. A buyer purchases a home without conducting a title search. Two years later, a defect is discovered in the title. What is the buyer's recourse?

    A.   Sue the seller under breach of warranty

    B.   Rescind the contract due to a mutual mistake

    C.   Place a lis pendens on the property

    D.   Acquire title insurance to cover the defect

Q4. A seller fails to disclose extensive termite damage while marketing a property. What legal principle governs this situation?

    A.   Caveat emptor

    B.   Escheat

    C.   Lis pendens

    D.   Res ipsa loquitor

Q5. What is the definition of an involuntary lien?

    A.   A lien intentionally filed by a creditor

    B.   A lien filed by a property owner against themselves

    C.   A lien granted voluntarily by a property owner

    D.   A lien arising by operation of law rather than consent

Q6. A property owner allows a neighbor to park in their driveway occasionally. What type of property interest has been created?

    A.   License

    B.   Adverse possession

    C.   Easement

    D.   Encroachment

Q7. Which of the following requires the MOST parties to convey?

    A.   Leasehold estate

    B.   Life estate

    C.   Fee simple absolute

    D.   Joint tenancy with right of survivorship

Q8. A property owner records an affidavit indicating they own a strip of land also claimed by a neighbor. What is this document called?

    A.   Lis pendens

    B.   Quitclaim deed

    C.   General warranty deed

    D.   Affidavit of adverse possession

Q9. What is the Statute of Frauds?

    A.   A law requiring contracts for goods over $500 to be in writing

    B.   A law setting the legal age for executing a contract

    C.   A law requiring land contracts to be in writing

    D.   A law establishing contract formalities for competent parties

Q10. A homebuyer purchases a home inspector's service. What guarantees regarding the home's quality are made?

    A.   Implied warranties from the inspection report

    B.   Expressed warranties from the seller

    C.   Guarantees inferred through the doctrine of caveat emptor

    D.   No guarantees are made beyond the service provided

Q11. A buyer purchases a home that unknowingly violates local zoning laws regarding setbacks. Who is responsible for bringing the property into compliance?

      A.   The seller

      B.   The buyer

      C.   The mortgage company

      D.   The zoning board

Q12. What is the main distinction between a special warranty deed and a general warranty deed?

      A.   Only a general warranty deed provides buyer protection from title claims.

      B.   A special warranty deed limits seller liability to the time they owned the property.

      C.   A special warranty deed provides more buyer protection than a general deed.

      D.   Only a special warranty deed guarantees unrestricted use of the property.

Q13. Which of the following violates the Equal Credit Opportunity Act?

      A.   Refusing to lend to unqualified applicants

      B.   Considering an applicant's marital status

      C.   Reviewing an applicant's debt-to-income ratio

      D.   Denying credit based on an applicant's race

Q14. A property owner allows a neighbor to store items in their shed temporarily. What interest has been created?

      A.   Joint tenancy

      B.   Tenancy in common

      C.   Executory interest

      D.   Bailment estate

Q15. What is the purpose of the Truth in Lending Act (TILA)?

      A.   To provide buyers with details on total borrowing costs

      B.   To require sellers to disclose all property defects

      C.   To establish minimum lending standards and practices

      D.   To regulate predatory and discriminatory lending

Q16. Which federal law prohibits housing discrimination based on family status?

    A.   The Fair Housing Act

    B.   The Home Mortgage Disclosure Act

    C.   The Equal Credit Opportunity Act

    D.   The Real Estate Settlement Procedures Act

Q17. What does the doctrine of equitable conversion establish?

    A.   That real estate contracts must be in writing to be enforceable

    B.   That buyers can seek reimbursement for improvements made

    C.   That buyers have equitable title upon signing a contract

    D.   That buyers must be given reasonable access to inspect the property

Q18. A property owner designates her spouse as the sole beneficiary in her will. At her death, how will the property transfer?

    A.   By descent

    B.   By device

    C.   By intestacy laws

    D.   Through adverse possession

Q19. What is the main difference between an installment land contract and a lease with the option to buy?

    A.   Only a lease with the option to buy involves monthly payments

    B.   The installment contract conveys equitable title before the conveyance

    C.   The lease with the option to buy includes a purchase option

    D.   The installment contract can be terminated without penalty

Q20. A property owner finds survey stakes showing a neighbor's garage encroaching on their land. Which action would establish a right to maintain the garage?

    A.   Asking for an easement

    B.   Withdrawing any objections

    C.   Applying for a zoning variance

    D.   Removing the encroaching garage

Q21. A home seller fails to disclose a known defect during the sale. What legal principle applies?

     A.   Quiet enjoyment

     B.   Caveat emptor

     C.   Fraudulent misrepresentation

     D.   Titles in derogation of common law

Q22. What is the definition of cloud in the title?

     A.   A defect in the legal ownership rights

     B.   An outstanding mortgage balance

     C.   A lien recorded against the property

     D.   A restriction on land use

Q23. A property owner records a new plat map correcting an error in the legal description of their lot. This is an example of:

     A.   Intestate succession

     B.   A correction deed

     C.   A lis pendens

     D.   A quitclaim deed

Q24. Which federal law requires lenders to provide a Good Faith Estimate of closing costs?

     A.   The Real Estate Settlement Procedures Act

     B.   The Equal Credit Opportunity Act

     C.   The Truth in Lending Act

     D.   The Fair Housing Act

Q25. A buyer purchases a home and then discovers the seller failed to disclose known roof leaks. What is the buyer's primary recourse?

     A.   File a lis pendens on the property

     B.   Rescind the purchase contract

     C.   Place a mechanic's lien on the home

     D.   Sue the seller for fraudulent misrepresentation

Q26. What does the implied warranty of habitability guarantee for rental tenants?

    A.   The landlord will make all requested repairs

    B.   The property will be move-in ready at lease signing

    C.   The property will be suitable for occupation

    D.   The landlord will maintain the property full-time

Q27. A property's ownership is transferred with its current deed and no amendments. What is this called?

    A.   Lis pendens

    B.   Quitclaim deed

    C.   Special warranty deed

    D.   General warranty deed

Q28. What is the main advantage of joint tenancy with the right of survivorship?

    A.   It avoids probate upon an owner's death

    B.   It provides greater legal protection than tenancy in common

    C.   It separates ownership interests in the property itself

    D.   It requires written consent from all owners to transfer interests

Q29. Which federal fair housing law introduced protected classes based on handicap and familial status?

    A.   The Civil Rights Act

    B.   The Fair Housing Amendment Act

    C.   The Housing Rights Act

    D.   The Equal Housing Opportunity Act

Q30. A property owner grants a cell phone company an easement to install a new tower. Which type of easement was created?

    A.   Appurtenant easement

    B.   Affirmative easement

    C.   Negative easement

    D.   Easement in gross

Q31. Which federal law regulates the lending process to ensure fairness and transparency?

      A.   The Equal Credit Opportunity Act

      B.   The Truth in Lending Act

      C.   The Real Estate Settlement Procedures Act

      D.   The Fair Housing Act

Q32. A property owner constructs a building that encroaches on the neighbor's land by mistake. Which doctrine would apply?

      A.   Adverse possession

      B.   Trespass

      C.   Escheat

      D.   De minimis

Q33. What is the definition of redlining?

      A.   Charging excessive fees to lower-income applicants

      B.   Providing special lending incentives to urban areas

      C.   Refusing services or loans within certain geographic areas

      D.   Basing decisions on an applicant's marital status

Q34. What is the main advantage of a land trust?

      A.   It allows shared ownership without joint liability

      B.   It avoids probate through rights of survivorship

      C.   It limits government control over private property

      D.   It provides a way to transfer ownership tax-free

Q35. Under which ownership arrangement does each owner have an undivided interest in the entire property?

      A.   Tenancy in common

      B.   Joint tenancy

      C.   Tenancy by the entirety

      D.   Community property

Q36. Which federal law regulates the disclosure of borrower information among financial institutions?

A.   The Fair Credit Reporting Act

B.   The Equal Credit Opportunity Act

C.   The Fair Debt Collection Practices Act

D.   The Gramm-Leach-Bliley Act

Q37. What is the difference between an agent and a broker in real estate?

A.   Only brokers can facilitate transactions, while agents cannot

B.   Agents work for brokers who represent the clients

C.   Brokers charge commissions, while agents charge flat fees

D.   Only agents can legally provide real estate services

Q38. What does the term "cloud on title" refer to?

A.   An unknown heir claiming ownership

B.   An unrecorded lien on the property

C.   A defect or uncertainty in the legal title

D.   The lender's security interest in the property

Q39. Which federal legislation prohibits housing discrimination based on sexual orientation or gender identity?

A.   The Civil Rights Act

B.   The Fair Housing Act

C.   The Home Mortgage Disclosure Act

D.   The Community Reinvestment Act

Quiz 2 Answer Key

1) Answer: B

Explanation: A general warranty deed guarantees that the seller rightfully holds a fee simple title and promises to defend the buyer against title claims. It does not warrant condition.

2) Answer: D

Explanation: Competent parties who are of legal age and sound mind are essential to create an enforceable contract. Consideration is also needed, but signatures and remedies are not.

3) Answer: D

Explanation: Without conducting a title search initially, the buyer cannot go after the seller later for title defects. The only recourse is a title insurance policy.

4) Answer: A

Explanation: Caveat emptor means "buyer beware" and governs real estate transactions, placing responsibility on the buyer to inspect the property and assume risk. Termite damage would not have to be voluntarily disclosed.

5) Answer: D

Explanation: Involuntary liens arise automatically rather than by agreement. They include tax liens, HOA liens, mechanic's liens, and other non-consensual encumbrances.

6) Answer: A

Explanation: A license grants temporary use rights but does not create a permanent property interest. Easements and encroachments involve interests in the land itself.

7) Answer: D

Explanation: Joint tenancy with the right of survivorship requires all joint tenants to consent to conveyance. The others only require the consent of the individual interest holder.

8) Answer: A

Explanation: A lis pendens gives constructive notice that a property is involved in pending litigation, forcing buyers to investigate the title dispute.

9) Answer: C

Explanation: The Statute of Frauds requires contracts concerning real property interests to be in writing to be enforceable. It does NOT apply to age or goods.

10) Answer: D

Explanation: Home inspectors only guarantee their limited service, not the home itself. They make no warranties, express or implied, about a home's quality.

11)   Answer: B

Explanation: The buyer assumes responsibility for property compliance and condition once the purchase is completed. The seller has no obligation after closing.

12)   Answer: B

Explanation: A special warranty deed limits the seller's liability to the time they owned the property, while a general warranty is broader.

13)   Answer: D

Explanation: Denying credit based on race, gender, marital status, etc., violates the Equal Credit Opportunity Act. Reviewing qualifications does not.

14)   Answer: D

Explanation: A bailment estate involves the temporary possession of personal (not real) property by someone other than the owner. No tenancy or future interest is created.

15)   Answer: A

Explanation: The Truth in Lending Act aims to provide transparency to borrowers about total lending costs through mandatory disclosures.

16)   Answer: A

Explanation: The Fair Housing Act prohibits housing discrimination based on race, color, religion, sex, family status, and national origin.

17)   Answer: C

Explanation: The doctrine of equitable conversion recognizes buyers as equitable owners with title rights once a contract is signed.

18)   Answer: B

Explanation: Transferring property to a designated beneficiary by will is called a transfer by device. Descent and intestacy involve situations without a will.

19)   Answer: C

Explanation: A lease with the option to buy contains a purchase option not in an installment land contract. The installment contract vests equitable ownership rights before legal conveyance occurs.

20)   Answer: B

Explanation: Failing to object to a known encroachment can lead to the encroacher acquiring the right to maintain the structure through prescriptive rights.

21)   Answer: C

Explanation: Failing to disclose a known material defect constitutes fraudulent misrepresentation, giving the buyer recourse against the seller.

22)   Answer: A

Explanation: A cloud on title is any defect in the legal ownership rights, such as an unknown heir claiming ownership interest. It is not the same as a lien itself.

23)   Answer: B

Explanation: A correction deed amends a defective or erroneous deed. A new plat map can correct legal description errors.

24)   Answer: A

Explanation: The Real Estate Settlement Procedures Act (RESPA) requires lenders to provide a Good Faith Estimate of closing costs to borrowers.

25)   Answer: D

Explanation: Failing to disclose known material defects constitutes fraudulent misrepresentation, giving the buyer a right to sue the seller for damages.

26)   Answer: C

Explanation: The implied warranty of habitability guarantees rental units will be fit for occupation, with basic utilities and services provided. It does not obligate landlords to make all repairs on demand.

27)   Answer: B

Explanation: A quitclaim deed is when a seller transfers a property to a buyer without making any or little amendments or additions.

28)   Answer: A

Explanation: Joint tenancy with right of survivorship avoids probate by automatically passing ownership to survivors upon death.

29)   Answer: B

Explanation: The Fair Housing Amendment Act added protected classes for handicap/disability and familial status.

30)   Answer: D

Explanation: An easement in gross directly benefits the holder, not another property. Utility easements are typically easements in gross.

31)   Answer: C

Explanation: The Real Estate Settlement Procedures Act (RESPA) governs the mortgage lending process to ensure upfront disclosure of costs and prohibit kickbacks in the process.

32)   Answer: D

Explanation: The de minimis doctrine allows minor encroachments made by accident to remain if removal would be impractical or burdensome compared to the scale.

33)   Answer: C

Explanation: Redlining refers to refusing loan or service applications based solely on the geographic location, often racially discriminatory.

34)   Answer: A

Explanation: A land trust allows shared ownership and management of land while limiting personal liability for the owners.

35)   Answer: B

Explanation: In joint tenancy, each owner has an equal undivided interest in the entire estate. Tenants in common have distinct fractional interests.

36)   Answer: D

Explanation: The Gramm-Leach-Bliley Act regulates financial institutions' use and disclosure of private borrower information.

37)   Answer: B

Explanation: Real estate agents work under brokers and represent clients on their behalf. Agents cannot practice independently.

38)   Answer: C

Explanation: A cloud on title is any defect or uncertainty about the legal ownership, like an unknown heir claiming rights. A lien itself is not a cloud on the title.

39)   Answer: B

Explanation: The Fair Housing Act prohibits discrimination based on race, color, national origin, religion, sex, familial status, and handicap. Courts have applied protections against sexual orientation and gender identity discrimination under the Act.

[Quiz 3 - For All Topics]

Q1. Which of the following is true about the brokerage relationship?

    A.   Brokers represent the interests of buyers or sellers, but not both in the same transaction

    B.   Brokers act solely as agents of the state licensing authorities

    C.   Brokers represent the interests of transaction stakeholders other than buyers and sellers

    D.   Brokers have no fiduciary responsibilities towards buyers or sellers

Q2. Which of the following violates fair housing laws? I. Refusing to rent to families with children II. Charging higher rents for tenants who are disabled III. Not allowing service animals in a rental property IV. Limiting showings based on an applicant's religion.

    A.   I and II only

    B.   II and IV only

    C.   I, II and IV

    D.   I, II, III and IV

Q3. Which of the following is required to legally change a property's zoning designation?

    A.   Public hearings before the zoning board

    B.   Approval by all neighborhood residents

    C.   Review by the local planning commission

    D.   A variance issued by the zoning administrator

Q4. Which of the following transfers an insured's interest in a property to the mortgage company to avoid foreclosure?

    A.   Short sale

    B.   Deed in lieu of foreclosure

    C.   Escheatment

    D.   Lis pendens

Q5. Which of the following types of listing agreements allow sellers to cooperate with other brokers?

    A.   Open

    B.   Exclusive right-to-sell

    C.   Exclusive agency

    D.   Multiple listing service

Q6. Which of the following is required for adverse possession to lead to legal ownership? I. Exclusive use II. Continued use over the statutory period III. Use without the owner's permission IV. Use that benefits the community

    A.   I, II, and III only

    B.   I, III, and IV only

    C.   II and IV only

    D.   I, II, III and IV

Q7. A property manager charges a 75% fee for securing tenants for an apartment building. This violates which law?

    A.   RESPA

    B.   Dodd-Frank Act

    C.   Sherman Antitrust Act

    D.   Fair Housing Act

Q8. Which federal agency enforces the majority of real estate laws and regulates mortgage lending?

    A.   Securities and Exchange Commission

    B.   Federal Housing Administration

    C.   Consumer Financial Protection Bureau

    D.   Federal Trade Commission

Q9. Which of the following transfers ownership from deceased persons to their heirs?

    A.   Descent

    B.   Devise

    C.   Severance

    D.   Alienation

Q10. A housing developer needs approval for zoning variances before construction can begin. What is the BEST course of action?

    A.   File a variance petition with the city

    B.   Request a zoning commission hearing

    C.   Seek a zoning exemption from city council

    D.   Apply for an administrative zoning waiver

Q11. Which of the following is true about mortgage assumptions?

    A.   The new buyer becomes obligated on the existing mortgage

    B.   Lenders are obligated to accept assumptions

    C.   Assumptions override due-on-sale clauses

    D.   Assumptions require repayment of the loan

Q12. Which of the following is true about land installment contracts? I. Buyers receive the title after all payments are made. II. Sellers retain the title until payment is complete. III. Buyers have equitable rights during the contract IV. Defaulting buyers lose all invested money and interest

    A.   I and II only

    B.   II and III only

    C.   I, II, and IV only

    D.   I, II, III and IV

Q13. Which federal law regulates appraisal processes?

    A.   The Real Estate Settlement Procedures Act

    B.   The Truth in Lending Act

    C.   The Equal Credit Opportunity Act

    D.   The Appraisal Independence Act

Q14. Which of the following is required for a real estate contract to be binding in court? I. Consideration II. Competent parties III. Lawful purpose IV. The appurtenance of the land

    A.   I, II, and III only

    B.   I, III, and IV only

    C.   II and IV only

    D.   I, II, III, and IV

Q15. Which of the following is true about the statute of fraud?

    A.   It sets the legal age for executing contracts

    B.   It requires real estate contracts to be written

    C.   It establishes contractual formalities

    D.   It voids contracts made under duress

Q16. A buyer purchases a house and then discovers zoning restrictions prohibit commercial use despite plans to put in a home office. The buyer should have:

      A.   Reviewed restrictive covenants and zoning ordinances

      B.   Conducted a title search before closing

      C.   Demanded express written warranties

      D.   Purchased an owner's title insurance policy

Q17. Which of the following transfers ownership from a deceased owner automatically when there is no will?

      A.   Intestacy

      B.   Descent

      C.   Device

      D.   Escheat

Q18. A married couple owns a home. Upon divorce, how can ownership be transferred to just one spouse?

      A.   File an affidavit of equitable interest

      B.   Record a quitclaim deed from the other spouse

      C.   Have the other spouse grant a life estate

      D.   File for partition with the court

Q19. Which federal law requires "Good Faith Estimates" of closing costs for mortgage applicants?

      A.   RESPA

      B.   TILA

      C.   HMDA

      D.   ECOA

Q20. A buyer purchased a home one week ago but just lost their job due to company downsizing. What is the buyer's BEST recourse?

      A.   Sue the former employer for equitable repossession

      B.   Attempt to rescind based on mutual mistake

      C.   Return the property and request compensatory damages

      D.   List it for sale and hope to break even quickly

Q21. Which federal law oversees appraisal standards for federally-backed mortgages?

    A.   FIRREA

    B.   TILA

    C.   RESPA

    D.   HMDA

Q22. Which of the following statements constitutes illegal steering under the Fair Housing Act?

    A.   Directing buyers to certain neighborhoods based on family size

    B.   Providing information about school rankings to buyers with children

    C.   Recommending units with handicap-accessible features

    D.   Following up quickly with pre-qualified protected group members

Q23. Which federal regulation requires monthly mortgage statements to show how payments are applied?

    A.   Regulation Z

    B.   Regulation X

    C.   Regulation D

    D.   Regulation C

Q24. A married couple owns a home. To avoid probate, they could transfer title to themselves as:

    A.   Joint tenants

    B.   Tenants in common

    C.   Community property owners

    D.   Lien holders

Q25. Which of the following is regulated under the Equal Credit Opportunity Act? I. Discrimination in lending   II.   Appraisal   standards   III.   Loan   officer   kickbacks IV. Mortgage servicing practices

    A.   I and IV only

    B.   I, II and III only

    C.   II, III, and IV only

    D.   I, II, III and IV

Q26. A buyer purchased a home with an adjustable-rate mortgage. How can they confirm the maximum interest rate?

    A.   Truth in Lending disclosure

    B.   RESPA servicing notice

    C.   Initial escrow statement

    D.   Closing cost estimate

Q27. Which federal law allows heirs to avoid capital gains taxes on inherited property?

    A.   Title VII

    B.   IRS Code Section 121

    C.   IRS Code Section 1041

    D.   IRS Code Section 1031

Q28. Which of the following statements constitutes a fraudulent misrepresentation in selling real estate?

    A.   Installing a new roof before listing the home

    B.   Stating that remodeling was professionally done

    C.   Describing the neighborhood as "friendly"

    D.   Saying there are no known defects without checking

Q29. Which federal law requires mortgage lenders to disclose borrower information to credit reporting agencies?

    A.   HMDA

    B.   GLBA

    C.   FCRA

    D.   FHAA

Q30. Which of the following violates the implied warranty of habitability for rental units? I. No hot water for a month. II. Occasional clogged drains III. Drafty windows IV. Difficulty controlling room temperature

    A.   I only

    B.   I and II only

    C.   II and IV only

    D.   I, II, III and IV

Q31. A buyer purchased a home with a balcony that encroaches on the neighbor's property by 2 feet. This is an example of:

      A.   A physical taking

      B.   Adverse possession

      C.   Zoning variance

      D.   De minimis encroachment

Q32. A property owner wants to subdivide land and sell parcels currently zoned agricultural. What is needed first?

      A.   Permission from nearby homeowners

      B.   A variance from the zoning board

      C.   To file a plat with the recorder's office

      D.   Rezoning from local planning authorities

Q33. What is the difference between an easement appurtenant and an easement in gross?

      A.   Appurtenant easements are written, while gross easements are not

      B.   In gross easements require consideration, while appurtenances do not

      C.   Appurtenant easements involve servient estates while in gross, do not

      D.   In gross easements are transferable while appurtenances are not

Q34. Which federal law prohibits loan originator compensation based on loan terms and conditions?

      A.   ECOA

      B.   HMDA

      C.   Dodd-Frank Act

      D.   SAFE Act

Q35. Which of the following statements constitutes redlining?

      A.   Refusing services in low-income neighborhoods

      B.   Charging higher interest rates to higher-risk applicants

      C.   Marketing preferentially to white suburban areas

      D.   Using credit scoring models to assess creditworthiness

Q36. A property owner suspects that a neighbor's newly built fence encroaches on their land. What is the FIRST step they should take?

        A.   File for an injunction.

        B.   Notify the neighbor in writing.

        C.   Survey the property line.

        D.   Report the neighbor to zoning officials.

Q37. Which method of holding title specifies an owner's intention to transfer their interest to a co-owner upon death?

        A.   Tenants in common

        B.   Tenancy by the entirety

        C.   Joint tenancy with right of survivorship

        D.   Community property

Q38. Which of the following violates RESPA restrictions on kickbacks?

        A.   Paying agents referral fees for each closed transaction

        B.   Giving loan officers gifts under $25 value frequently

        C.   Buying leads and referrals from builders and realtors

        D.   Accepting appraisal services at a reasonable market value

Q39. A property owner wants to build a fence that exceeds height limits in local zoning codes. What is needed?

        A.   An authorized variance

        B.   To file an encroachment exception

        C.   Approval from neighbors

        D.   To notify the zoning board

Q40. Which federal law regulates the use and disclosure of consumer financial information?

        A.   HMDA

        B.   GLBA

        C.   ECOA

        D.   FDCPA

Quiz 3 Answer Key

1)   Answer: A

Explanation: Brokers represent the interests of either buyers or sellers in a transaction but cannot represent both parties in the same transaction under agency laws.

2)   Answer: D

Explanation: All the actions described violate fair housing laws by discriminating against protected classes.

3)   Answer: A

Explanation: Zoning reclassifications require public hearings to allow input from affected parties before approval.

4)   Answer: B

Explanation: A deed in lieu of foreclosure transfers title to the lender to avoid foreclosure. A short sale sells to a third party.

5)   Answer: C

Explanation: Exclusive agency listings allow sellers to cooperate with other brokers, while exclusive right-to-sell listings do not.

6)   Answer: A

Explanation: The key elements for adverse possession are open, continuous, adverse use over the statutory period. Benefitting the community is not required.

7)   Answer: C

Explanation: The excessive fee violates antitrust laws prohibiting anti-competitive business practices. It does not fall under RESPA, Dodd-Frank, or the Fair Housing Act.

8)   Answer: C

Explanation: The CFPB enforces most federal real estate and mortgage lending laws and regulations.

9)   Answer: A

Explanation: The transfer of property to heirs when the owner dies intestate is called descent. The device is transferred by will.

10)   Answer: B

Explanation: To obtain zoning variances, a public hearing before the zoning board is typically required.

11)   Answer: A

Explanation: When a mortgage is assumed, the buyer takes over responsibility for the seller's existing loan. The lender must approve assumptions.

12) Answer: B

Explanation: Sellers retain title until all payments are made, while buyers gain equitable interest. Buyers do not get the title until fully paid.

13) Answer: D

Explanation: The Appraisal Independence Act regulates appraisal standards and independence, prohibiting conflicts of interest.

14) Answer: A

Explanation: Valid real estate contracts require competent parties, lawful purpose, and consideration. Appurtenance is for restrictive covenants.

15) Answer: B

Explanation: The statute of frauds requires real estate contracts to be in writing to be enforceable. It does not govern age or duress.

16) Answer: A

Explanation: Reviewing zoning ordinances and restrictions would have revealed the commercial use prohibition.

17) Answer: B

Explanation: When an owner dies intestate, ownership transfers to heirs by descent automatically based on state law.

18) Answer: B

Explanation: The other spouse can transfer interest through a quitclaim deed. The other methods would not convey full interest.

19) Answer: A

Explanation: The Real Estate Settlement Procedures Act requires Good Faith Estimates of closing costs.

20) Answer: D

Explanation: The buyer has no grounds to unwind the contract but can try to sell to avoid losses.

21) Answer: A

Explanation: FIRREA establishes appraisal standards for lenders making loans backed by federally related entities.

22) Answer: A

Explanation: Steering buyers to certain areas based on protected class status violates fair housing laws.

23) Answer: B

Explanation: Regulation X under RESPA contains rules on monthly mortgage statements.

24) Answer: A

Explanation: Joint tenancy allows the surviving spouse to automatically inherit the property outside probate.

25) Answer: A

Explanation: The ECOA governs lending discrimination. Appraisals, kickbacks, and servicing are under other regulations.

26) Answer: A

Explanation: Maximum rate information is disclosed on Truth in Lending statements provided to mortgage borrowers.

27) Answer: C

Explanation: Section 1041 of the tax code provides capital gains tax exemptions when property passes from a deceased person to an heir.

28) Answer: D

Explanation: Representing no known defects without checking constitutes fraud if defects are found. Other statements are opinion or puffing.

29) Answer: C

Explanation: The Fair Credit Reporting Act requires lenders to provide borrower payment information to credit reporting agencies.

30) Answer: A

Explanation: Extended loss of hot water violates the habitability warranty. Minor issues typically do not.

31) Answer: D

Explanation: Minor encroachments are typically allowed under the de minimis rule. It does not transfer title.

32) Answer: D

Explanation: Before subdividing agricultural land, rezoning for residential use would be required.

33) Answer: C

Explanation: An easement appurtenant benefits the dominant estate, while an easement in gross benefits the easement owner directly.

34) Answer: D

Explanation: The SAFE Act prohibits loan officer commissions based on loan terms as a conflict of interest.

35)   Answer: C

Explanation: Marketing preferentially by demographics constitutes redlining, which is illegal. Risk-based pricing is allowed.

36)   Answer: C

Explanation: Confirming the property line location via survey should be the first step taken.

37)   Answer: C

Explanation: Joint tenancy with the right of survivorship expresses intent for the interest to pass automatically to the other owner(s) upon death.

38)   Answer: A

Explanation: Paying or receiving any fees or kickbacks for referrals violates RESPA restrictions.

39)   Answer: A

Explanation: A variance specifically allows exceptions to zoning ordinances if certain criteria are met and approved.

40)   Answer: B

Explanation: The Gramm-Leach-Bliley Act regulates financial institutions' use of private consumer financial data.

Chapter 12: Real Estate Math Workbook

Real estate transactions involve a significant amount of math, from calculating commissions to understanding loan amortizations and property taxes. Having strong math skills is essential for real estate agents to accurately determine costs, profits, and affordability for their clients. This chapter will provide a deep dive into the key math concepts and calculations needed for the real estate salesperson exam and professional practice. With step-by-step examples, sample problems, and exercises, you will build proficiency in real estate math. Mastering these crucial skills will instill confidence for both passing the licensing exam and launching a successful career in real estate.

Commission Calculations

Commissions serve as the primary source of income for real estate agents. They are typically calculated as a percentage of the home's sale price and split between the listing and buyer's agents. Agents must understand how to accurately determine commission amounts based on the agreed-upon commission rate.

Key Commission Terminology

- Listing agent: Represents the home seller and markets the property for sale
- Buyer's Agent: Represents the home buyer to negotiate purchase terms
- Commission rate: Agreed percentage of the sales price paid to agents, often between 5-6%
- Commission split: How the commission is divided between listing and buyer's agents, traditionally 50/50

Commission Formula

Total Commission = Sale Price x Commission Rate

Individual Commission = Total Commission x Commission Split

For example:

- Sale Price: $500,000
- Commission Rate: 5%
- Commission Split: 50% listing agent, 50% buyer's agent

Total Commission = $500,000 x 0.05 = $25,000

Listing Agent Commission = $25,000 x 0.50 = $12,500 Buyer's Agent Commission = $25,000 x 0.50 = $12,500

Practice Problems

1. Sale Price: $425,000, Commission Rate: 6%, Commission Split: 60% listing agent, 40% buyer's agent

2. Sale Price: $650,000, Commission Rate: 4%, Commission Split: 65% listing agent, 35% buyer's agent

3. Sale Price: $340,000, Commission Rate: 5.5%, Commission Split: 70% listing agent, 30% buyer's agent

Answers

1. Total Commission = $425,000 x 0.06 = $25,500 Listing Agent = $25,500 x 0.60 = $15,300 Buyer's Agent = $25,500 x 0.40 = $10,200

2. Total Commission = $650,000 x 0.04 = $26,000 Listing Agent = $26,000 x 0.65 = $16,900 Buyer's Agent = $26,000 x 0.35 = $9,100

3. Total Commission = $340,000 x 0.055 = $18,700 Listing Agent = $18,700 x 0.70 = $13,090 Buyer's Agent = $18,700 x 0.30 = $5,610

Loan Interest and Amortization

Understanding loan interest and amortization is key for real estate agents to accurately depict financing terms for clients. Loan interest refers to the additional amount paid above the original loan principal to borrow the funds. Amortization is the process of gradually paying off a loan over time through fixed payments.

Key Terms Include

- Principal: Original loan amount borrowed
- Interest: Additional cost of borrowing money, usually denoted as an annual percentage rate (APR)
- Monthly payment: Fixed scheduled payment amount for loan repayment
- Amortization: Repayment of loan principal and interest through equal monthly installments over the loan term

Interest Formula

Annual Interest = Principal x APR

Monthly Interest = Annual Interest / 12 months

For example, on a 30-year $300,000 loan at 5% APR:

Annual Interest = $300,000 x 0.05 = $15,000

Monthly Interest = $15,000 / 12 months = $1,250

Monthly Payment Formula

$M = P [i(1 + i)^n] / [(1 + i)^n - 1]$

Where: M = Monthly Payment P = Principal Loan Amount i = Monthly Interest Rate (APR divided by 12) n = Number of Payments (Months)

Using the previous example, the monthly payment is:

i = 0.05 / 12 = 0.00417 n = 360 months

M = $300,000 [0.00417(1 + 0.00417)^360] / [(1 + 0.00417)^360 – 1] M = $1,432

Practice Problems

1. Calculate the monthly payment for a $225,000 loan at 4.5% APR for 30 years.

2. Calculate the total interest paid over the life of a $175,000 loan at 3.8% APR for 15 years.

3. Calculate the monthly payment and total interest for a $200,000 loan at 6% APR for 20 years.

Answers

1. i = 0.045 / 12 = 0.00375 n = 360 months M = $1,053

2. Total Interest = $175,000 x 0.038 x 15 = $98,850

3. i = 0.06 / 12 = 0.005 n = 240 months M = $1,332 Total Interest = $200,000 x 0.06 x 20 = $240,000

Property Tax Calculations

Property taxes vary by location and are based on the assessed value of a home. Real estate agents must understand how to calculate property taxes to analyze carrying costs for clients.

Key Terminology Includes

- Assessed value: Value placed on a property by the local tax authority to calculate taxes
- Tax rate: The amount per $100 of assessed value owed in property taxes
- Assessment ratio: Ratio between assessed and market values (often ranges between 80-100%)

Property Tax Formula

Annual Taxes = (Assessed Value / 100) x Tax Rate

For example, on a home with:

- Market Value: $350,000
- Assessment Ratio: 90%
- Assessed Value: $350,000 x 0.90 = $315,000
- Tax Rate: 1.25%

Annual Taxes = ($315,000 / 100) x 0.0125 = $3,937

Note assessment ratios, tax rates, and payment schedules can vary significantly by location. Agents must understand the methodology and specifics for each region.

Practice Problems

1. Calculate the annual property taxes on a home with a market value of $285,000 and a 95% assessment ratio in a district with a 1.8% tax rate.

2. Calculate the annual property taxes on a home with an assessed value of $205,000 and a 1.3% tax rate, paid biannually.

3. Calculate the monthly escrow payment for a home with an assessed value of $260,000, a 1.1% tax rate, and taxes paid monthly through an escrow account.

Answers

1. Assessed Value = $285,000 x 0.95 = $270,750 Annual Taxes = ($270,750 / 100) x 0.018 = $4,873

2. Annual Taxes = ($205,000 / 100) x 0.013 = $2,665 Biannual Payment = $2,665 / 2 = $1,332

3. Annual Taxes = ($260,000 / 100) x 0.011 = $2,860 Monthly Escrow = $2,860 / 12 = $238

Chapter 13: Final Mock Exam

Instructions and Timing

This final mock exam is designed to simulate the actual licensing exam you will take to become a real estate salesperson. It contains the same number of questions, time limits, and topics covered on the real licensing exam. Treat this practice test as if it were the real thing!

The exam is divided into two sections:

National Section: Contains 50 multiple-choice questions that cover general real estate concepts and laws found in all states. You will have 55 minutes to complete this section.

State-Specific Section: Contains 40 multiple-choice questions related to state-specific real estate laws and regulations. You will have 30 minutes to complete this section.

It is important to work through the exam sections sequentially, as you would on the actual exam. Be sure to keep track of time and do not go over the allotted time per section. Budget your time wisely so you can complete all questions.

Find a quiet space to take this practice exam and avoid any distractions. Have a timer handy to keep track of the time limits. You may use a basic calculator, but no other outside resources are permitted.

Read each question carefully and select the best answer. Try not to change your answers once selected. Only mark questions you are unsure of to revisit later if time permits.

Your goal is to achieve a passing score. On the actual exam, state-specific passing scores vary, but you generally need to correctly answer 60-75% of the questions to pass. Thoroughly review the explanations for any missed questions. This will help strengthen your knowledge as you continue preparing for the big day.

Let's get started! Good luck!

Multiple Choice Questions: National Section

Q1. Which of the following best describes the bundle of legal rights associated with property ownership?

A. Lien

B. Estate

C. Escrow

D. Easement

Q2. A married couple wishes to sell their home. They own the property as tenants in the entirety. Which statement does BEST describe how they hold title?

A. Each spouse has a separate, undivided ownership interest in the property.

B. Each spouse owns an undivided one-half interest in the property.

C. Each spouse owns the property jointly and entirely with rights of survivorship.

D. The husband owns a full interest in the property by virtue of being named first on the deed.

Q3. A real estate licensee is asked to represent a seller in the sale of a commercial property. The licensee should FIRST:

A. Explain the listing agreement terms to the seller

B. Have the seller complete a seller's disclosure form

C. Request financial documentation from the seller

D. Verify the seller has legal authority to sell the property

Q4. Which of the following Fair Housing Act prohibitions pertains to advertising real property?

A. Blockbusting

B. Redlining

C. Steering

D. Publishing discriminatory notices/statements

Q5. A lender appraises a property at $300,000 before approving a mortgage. If the appraisal sets the value at 20% higher than the property's actual market value, what is the property's MOST LIKELY market value?

    A. $240,000

    B. $250,000

    C. $260,000

    D. $270,000

Q6. A lease agreement states the tenant must vacate the property after giving proper notice equal to the number of days in the rental period. If rent is paid monthly, how much notice must the tenant provide?

    A. 3 days

    B. 30 days

    C. 60 days

    D. 90 days

Q7. Which of the following liens would have FIRST priority in the event of a foreclosure?

    A. Mortgage lien

    B. Mechanic's lien

    C. Tax lien

    D. Judgment lien

Q8. A buyer purchases a home for $250,000 with a 20% down payment. If the buyer must pay 4 discount points on the mortgage loan, how much are the points?

    A. $1,000

    B. $2,000

    C. $3,750

    D. $5,000

Q9. Which of the following violates the REAL ID Act's requirements for identification documents?

    A. Driver's license shows full legal name

    B. Social security card shows signature

    C. Birth certificate shows issue date

    D. Passport shows nationality

Q10.   A couple is considering buying a home priced at $350,000. Their monthly debt obligations total $2,500. If their back-end debt-to-income ratio cannot exceed 45%, what is the MINIMUM pre-tax income they must have to qualify?

A. $6,250
B. $6,666
C. $7,000
D. $7,500

Q11.   All of the following are required presale disclosures to a prospective buyer EXCEPT:

A.   Seller's Property Disclosure Statement
B.   Lead-Based Paint Disclosure
C.   State Guide to Environmental Hazards
D.   Homeowners Association Bylaws

Q12.   A lease agreement contains an exculpatory clause outlining conditions under which the landlord is NOT liable for injuries occurring on the property. Which statement is TRUE about this clause?

A.   It is illegal in all jurisdictions.
B.   It can exempt the landlord from liability for negligence.
C.   It can only limit tenant liability for negligence.
D.   It cannot limit liability for intentional landlord misconduct.

Q13.   Which of the following activities is permitted for real estate licensees under RESPA anti-kickback regulations?

A.   Giving a gift card to a mortgage lender, making monthly referrals
B.   Accepting a software subscription from a title company partner
C.   Receiving a meal from an affiliated home inspector
D.   Providing promotional items to generate leads and referrals

Q14. A couple purchases a property from a seller who fails to disclose sizable defects. The title company does NOT inform the couple of recorded easements on the property. If the couple sues for nondisclosure, who will MOST LIKELY be found negligent?

A. Title company only

B. Seller only

C. Seller and title company jointly

D. Seller primarily, title company secondarily

Q15. A property owner grants a real estate licensee exclusive right to sell her home. All of the following are TRUE about this arrangement EXCEPT:

A. It must establish a definite expiration date.

B. Other licensees may still be solicited to purchase the property.

C. The brokerage must advertise and promote the listing.

D. The owner can be liable for brokerage commission if sold during the term.

Q16. Which of the following violates advertising rules for real estate brokerages under the Fair Housing Act?

A. "Contact John Smith for a free market analysis."

B. "Smith & Brown Real Estate Services"

C. "We proudly serve first-time home buyers."

D. "Specializing in luxury hillside homes."

Q17. A homeowner is delinquent on mortgage payments. The lender initiates foreclosure proceedings and sells the property at auction. Which of the following is TRUE about any foreclosure surplus?

A. It is retained by the mortgage lender.

B. It is paid to subsequent lien holders.

C. It is returned to the homeowner.

D. It is transferred to tax authorities.

Q18.   Which of the following scenarios allows for the legal termination of an agency relationship by the agent/brokerage?

A.   The client moves out of the brokerage's service area.

B.   The brokerage files for bankruptcy.

C.   The client repeatedly fails to pay service fees.

D.   The client is convicted of mortgage fraud.

Q19.   To qualify as an accredited real estate investor, which of the following must be TRUE?

A.   Individual net worth exceeds $1 million.

B.   Individual income exceeds $200K/year.

C.   Entity net worth exceeds $5 million.

D.   All of the above.

Q20.   Which of the following transfers a deceased person's interest in a property jointly owned with the right of survivorship?

A.   Transfer on death deed

B.   Beneficiary deed

C.   Surviving joint tenant acquires interest by law.

D.   Interest is subject to probate.

Q21.   An owner sells a commercial property for $1.2 million. The brokerage's commission rate is 6%. How much is the brokerage's commission?

A. $36,000

B. $48,000

C. $60,000

D. $72,000

Q22.   A landlord offers a commercial tenant free rent for 2 months if the tenant signs a 3-year lease. How would this arrangement MOST likely be classified?

A.   Discounted rent

B.   Liquidated damages

C.   Sublease concession

D.   Lease inducement

Q23. Brokers often use the abbreviation "ENC" in listing advertisements. What does this abbreviation stand for?

A. Environmental Conditions

B. Estimated New Construction

C. Exclusive Negotiating Contract

D. Easements Not Clear

Q24. An owner sells a rental property valued at $400,000 to his son for only $250,000. The owner does NOT report the transaction to the IRS. This scenario is an example of:

A. Assessed value fraud

B. Appraisal fraud

C. Mortgage fraud

D. Tax fraud

Q25. A buyer offers $275,000 for a home listed at $260,000. The seller counteroffers $280,000. The potential gross commission is 6%. How much commission will the listing brokerage earn if the buyer accepts the counteroffer?

A. $9,240

B. $12,320

C. $15,400

D. $16,800

Q26. Which of the following violates the provisions of the Equal Credit Opportunity Act?

A. Requesting a joint applicant's income information

B. Denying credit to an applicant delinquent on prior obligations

C. Considering an applicant's age

D. Verifying an applicant's employment

Q27. A state's commissioner of real estate has the authority to do all of the following EXCEPT:

A. Investigate alleged violations of license law

B. Suspend or revoke real estate licenses

C. Appraise property values for tax purposes

D. Determine qualifications for licensure

Q28. Which of the following entities insures a property owner's title against defects and liens?

A. Mortgage lender

B. Escrow company

C. Title insurer

D. Property inspector

Q29. A property owner dies intestate with no spouse or children. Who inherits the property according to laws of descent and distribution?

A. Cousins

B. Parents

C. Siblings

D. Grandparents

Q30. Which of the following activities does NOT require a real estate license?

A. Purchasing property for one's own investment

B. Managing a 50-unit apartment building

C. Renting two duplex units owned by the same investor

D. Listing a commercial property for sale

Q31. A married couple owns their home as community property. If one spouse dies, ownership of the entire property will:

A. Transfer to the surviving spouse.

B. Be divided equally among heirs.

C. Be sold and proceeds split between heirs.

D. Require appraisal to determine new ownership.

Q32. Which of the following real estate investments would be exempt from securities registration requirements?

A. REIT with 75 total shareholders

B. Limited partnership with 15 limited partners

C. LLC with non-accredited co-owners

D. Corporation with 35 preferred stockholders

Q33. A buyer purchases a home that is subject to an existing oil and gas lease. The lease will:

A. Prevent the buyer from obtaining title insurance.

B. Cloud the title but remain in effect.

C. Transfer to the buyer upon sale.

D. Be nullified upon transfer of ownership.

Q34. Which of the following violates agency requirements of loyalty and disclosure?

A. As a dual agent, encouraging negotiation between both parties

B. Advising the seller to list at a higher price than recommended

C. Disclosing all material facts known about a property to a buyer

D. Providing comparable sales data only to the seller

Q35. Which of the following is classified as voluntary unemployment?

A. Quitting a job without new employment

B. Being terminated for cause

C. Getting laid off from a position

D. Leaving work due to disability

Q36. Under which type of listing agreement does the seller retain the right to sell the property?

A. Open listing

B. Exclusive agency listing

C. Exclusive right-to-sell listing

D. Net listing

Q37. Which of the following would NOT be an incidental boundary line encroachment?

A. Small portion of the neighbor's driveway on the property

B. Underground septic system extending across the lot line

C. Fence built several feet over the boundary line

D. Eaves overhanging slightly across the property line

Q38.   A landlord rents out a single-family residence and lives in another state. This arrangement BEST describes which type of property?

A.   Commercial

B.   Industrial

C.   Nonresidential investment

D.   Residential investment

Q39.   A borrower with an adjustable-rate mortgage receives notice that the interest rate will increase. The lender must provide the notice:

A.   30 days before increase

B.   60 days before the increase

C.   90 days before increase

D.   120 days before increase

Q40.   A couple purchases a home for $285,000 by assuming the seller's existing mortgage and obtaining a new second mortgage. What type of sales transaction occurred?

A.   Short sale

B.   Foreclosure sale

C.   Sale subject to existing financing

D.   All cash sale

Q41.   Which of the following statements constitutes actionable misrepresentation by a real estate licensee?

A.   "This property holds tremendous potential!"

B.   "Interest rates are still at all-time lows."

C.   "I know the seller well - this home is a great investment."

D.   "The roof was replaced last year."

Q42. A property owner wants to subdivide a parcel of land and develop it into a new subdivision. This plan should FIRST be submitted to the local:

A. Tax assessor's office

B. Zoning board

C. Planning commission

D. Association of Realtors

Q43. Which of the following transfers ownership of real property without a deed?

A. Testamentary will

B. Intestate succession

C. Divorce court order

D. All of the above

Q44. A lender denies a mortgage application after reviewing the applicant's debt-to-income ratios and down payment amount. What is the PRIMARY legal issue here?

A. Defamation

B. Fraud

C. Discrimination

D. Nondisclosure

Q45. A property owner adds a 20x30 ft. addition to a home without obtaining the required permit or adhering to the code. This scenario is an example of which legal concept?

A. Patent defect

B. Latent defect

C. Legal nonconforming use

D. Zoning variance

Q46. A buyer purchases a commercial warehouse subject to the existing tenant's lease. Under which doctrine does the buyer assume obligations per the lease terms?

A. Caveat emptor

B. De facto agency

C. Substitution of trustee

D. Privity of estate

Q47. A brokerage firm engages in which of the following ILLEGAL practices under RESPA?

A. Accepting IT services from a title company affiliate

B. Buying leads data from an industry marketing company

C. Sharing office space with a partner lender

D. Displaying affiliate branding/logos on office materials

Q48. Which of the following injuries is covered under worker's compensation insurance?

A. Food poisoning at an office event

B. Car accident driving to showing

C. Dog bite at listed property

D. Fall slipping on ice at listing

Q49. According to the Fair Housing Act, which of the following is classified as a reasonable accommodation?

A. Allowing an assistance animal in a no-pet building.

B. Providing a reserved accessible parking space.

C. Permitting a live-in personal caregiver.

D. All of the above.

Q50. A broker lists a property at a 5% commission. She hires an agent from another brokerage to show the property to interested buyers. How will the commission MOST likely be divided?

A. 5% to listing broker, 0% to agent

B. 2.5% to listing broker, 2.5% to agent

C. 3% to listing broker, 2% to agent

D. 4% to listing broker, 1% to agent

Answer Key

1) **Correct Answer: B**

Explanation: The bundle of legal rights associated with property ownership is known as an estate. This bundle of rights defines the owner's rights, privileges, and limitations to use the property. A lien, escrow, and easement represent more limited property rights or interests.

2) **Correct Answer: C**

Explanation: Tenants by the entirety is a special form of joint tenancy available only to married couples. Each spouse owns the property jointly and entirely with rights of survivorship. If one spouse dies, the other automatically inherits full ownership. Answers A and B describe other forms of joint tenancy. Answer D incorrectly assumes the husband has priority.

3) **Correct Answer: D**

Explanation: The FIRST step a licensee should take when representing a new seller is to verify their legal authority to sell the property. This ensures the licensee is working with the actual property owner or authorized representative before disclosing confidential information or entering into a listing agreement. Answers A, B, and C are important but premature until the seller's authority is validated.

4) **Correct Answer: D**

Explanation: The Fair Housing Act prohibits publishing any discriminatory notice, statement, or advertisement related to the sale or rental of real estate. Blockbusting, redlining, and steering are other Fair Housing violations but do not directly pertain to advertising.

5) **Correct Answer: A**

Explanation: If the appraised value ($300,000) is 20% higher than the actual market value, the market value can be calculated as follows:

$300,000 / 1.20 = $250,000 (appraised value divided by 1.20)

$250,000 x 0.80 = $200,000 (market value is 80% of appraised value)

Therefore, the property's most likely market value is $240,000.

6) **Correct Answer: B**

Explanation: If rent is paid monthly, the rental period is one month. Therefore, proper notice would be equal to 30 days (the number of days in the rental period).

7) **Correct Answer: C**

Explanation: Tax liens typically have first priority, followed by mortgage liens, mechanic's liens, and judgment liens. This reflects the relative importance given to each type of claim. Unpaid property taxes threaten a municipality's functioning, so tax liens are given the highest status.

8) Correct Answer: C

Explanation: Discount points are prepaid interest charged as a percentage of the mortgage loan. Each point equals 1% of the loan amount.

Loan amount = $250,000 purchase price - $50,000 down payment = $200,000

4 points x 1% of $200,000 = 0.04 x $200,000 = $8,000

Therefore, the points total $3,750.

9) Correct Answer: B

Explanation: Under the REAL ID Act, Social Security cards cannot display any information other than name, number, and issue/expiration date. Signatures are prohibited. Answer B is the only violation listed.

10) Correct Answer: B

Explanation: The back-end (total) debt ratio includes all monthly debt payments, including mortgage: Monthly Debts = $2,500 Max Total Debt Ratio = 45%

$2,500 / 45% = $5,555.55 minimum monthly income $5,555.55 x 12 months = $66,666 annual pre-tax income

Therefore, the minimum income is $6,666/month.

11) Correct Answer: D

Explanation: Seller's Property, Lead-Based Paint, and State Environmental Hazard disclosures are required for residential real estate transactions. Homeowners association bylaws are not mandatory presale disclosures. The seller may voluntarily provide them.

12) Correct Answer: D

Explanation: Exculpatory clauses cannot exempt a landlord from liability resulting from intentional or reckless misconduct. They may only limit liability stemming from ordinary negligence, as answer B states. The clauses are not categorically illegal, nor do they pertain to tenant conduct.

13) Correct Answer: D

Explanation: RESPA permits giving/accepting promotional items of nominal value to generate leads or referrals. The other options either provide services/benefits selective to referral partners (violation of anti-kickback regulations) or are not nominal in value.

14) Correct Answer: D

Explanation: The seller had a duty to disclose known defects and would be primarily liable for nondisclosure negligence. However, the title company also negligently failed to inform buyers of easements. The seller bears principal responsibility, but the title company may share secondary liability.

15) Correct Answer: B

Explanation: Option B is false. An exclusive right-to-sell listing reserves transaction rights exclusively for the listing brokerage. The owner cannot solicit or hire other brokers to sell the property during the listing term without penalty.

16) Correct Answer: D

Explanation: Advertising specialization in only luxury properties could discourage potential buyers based on income level, violating Fair Housing. The other statements don't imply discriminatory preference.

17) Correct Answer: C

Explanation: Any surplus funds after paying off liens/fees in foreclosure sales are returned to the original homeowner. Surplus is not kept by lenders, paid to other lien holders, or given to tax authorities.

18) Correct Answer: C

Explanation: Repeated nonpayment of earned fees provides grounds for a brokerage to terminate agency representation of a client. The other scenarios do not legally allow the brokerage to end the relationship unilaterally.

19) Correct Answer: D

Explanation: To qualify as accredited, an individual must meet net worth OR income requirements. Entities must meet the net worth standard. All answer choices are mandatory accreditation criteria.

20) Correct Answer: C

Explanation: With joint tenancy with the right of survivorship, the surviving co-owner automatically inherits the deceased's interest. No deed transfer is needed, unlike transfer/beneficiary deeds, which require recording. Interest does not pass through probate.

21) Correct Answer: C

Explanation: Commission = Price x Rate

Price = $1,200,000 Rate = 6%

$1,200,000 x 0.06 = $72,000

Therefore, the commission is $60,000.

22) Correct Answer: D

Explanation: Offering free rent to induce a tenant to sign a long-term lease is considered a lease inducement or concession. It is not a sublease or liquidated damages, nor is rent simply discounted.

23) Correct Answer: C

Explanation: ENC is a common shorthand for an Exclusive Negotiating Contract, an agreement giving a potential buyer time to evaluate a property before entering a purchase contract. It does NOT involve easements, construction, or environment.

24) Correct Answer: D

Explanation: By underreporting the sale price to a family member, the seller is committing tax fraud or intentional misrepresentation to the IRS to avoid capital gains taxes owed. There is no mortgage, appraisal, or assessed value manipulation.

25) Correct Answer: C

Explanation:

Sale price = $280,000 Commission rate = 6%

$280,000 x 0.06 = $16,800 total commission

Listing brokerage earns 60% of commission: $16,800 x 0.60 = $15,400

Therefore, the listing broker will earn $15,400.

26) Correct Answer: C

Explanation: The ECOA prohibits lenders from considering age when evaluating applicants.

27) Correct Answer: C

Explanation: Real estate commissioners administer licensing but do not perform property appraisals. That is the role of a town assessor, not the commissioner.

28) Correct Answer: C

Explanation: A title insurer provides title insurance protecting the owner from title defects, liens, and other issues. Mortgage lenders, escrow companies, and inspectors do not offer insurance on the title itself.

29) Correct Answer: B

Explanation: If an intestate decedent has no spouse or descendants, parents are next in line to inherit under descent and distribution laws. More distant relatives like cousins, siblings, or grandparents have lower priority.

30) Correct Answer: A

Explanation: Purchasing one's own real estate does NOT require an agent/broker license. The other activities all constitute real estate services for third parties that mandate a license.

31) Correct Answer: A

Explanation: With community property, the entire estate passes directly to the surviving spouse when one spouse dies. It does NOT get divided or require appraisal for new ownership.

32) Correct Answer: B

Explanation: Securities laws exempt limited partnerships with fewer than 35 unaccredited partners. The other examples exceed exemption limits for shareholders/partners.

33) Correct Answer: B

Explanation: Preexisting leases remain in effect through ownership transfers. The lease clouds but does not block title insurance and does not get nullified or transferred.

34) Correct Answer: D

Explanation: Withholding comparable sales from a buyer violates disclosure duty. Answer A represents appropriate dual agency conduct. Answers B and C demonstrate loyalty.

35) Correct Answer: A

Explanation: Voluntary unemployment involves quitting a job without having new employment lined up already. Disability, layoffs, and termination for cause are involuntary.

36) Correct Answer: B

Explanation: Unlike an exclusive right-to-sell agreement, an exclusive agency listing allows the property seller to sell independently without owing the listing brokerage a commission.

37) Correct Answer: C

Explanation: A fence built significantly over the boundary line is more than an incidental minor encroachment. The other examples are acceptable incidental encroachments.

38) Correct Answer: D

Explanation: A single-family home used as a rental property represents residential rental real estate, classified as a residential investment property. It is NOT commercial, industrial, or nonresidential.

39) Correct Answer: C

Explanation: Lenders must notify ARM borrowers of rate adjustments 90 days in advance, allowing time to react and budget accordingly before monthly payments rise.

40) Correct Answer: C

Explanation: The buyers purchased the property subject to the seller's existing first mortgage, which is an example of a sale subject to financing. It does NOT involve paying all cash, foreclosure, or a short sale.

41) Correct Answer: D

Explanation: Misrepresenting a material property fact like the roof's age constitutes misrepresentation. General statements in A, B, and C are puffery, opinions, or cannot be proven false.

42) Correct Answer: C

Explanation: Proposed subdivisions must first go through the local planning commission for review and approval before other steps like zoning changes. The planning commission governs development.

43) Correct Answer: D

Explanation: ownership can transfer without a deed through wills, intestate succession, and divorce decrees. All options can affect conveyance upon death or divorce without requiring a new deed.

44) Correct Answer: C

Explanation: By considering DTI and down payment, the lender may be discriminating against applicants with limited income/assets. This raises potential discrimination concerns, not fraud, defamation, or disclosure violations.

45) Correct Answer: B

Explanation: Unpermitted construction that violates the building code represents a latent defect. It exists but is not obvious to observers without inspection. A zoning variance was not obtained.

46) Correct Answer: D

Explanation: Privity of the estate binds successors in interest, like new buyers, to existing lease terms. Caveat emptor, de facto agency, and substitution of trustee do not apply.

47) Correct Answer: A

Explanation: Accepting services like IT support from affiliates violates RESPA anti-kickback provisions. The other actions are legal and permissible arrangements.

48) Correct Answer: D

Explanation: Injuries sustained on the job, like a fall at a listing, are covered by worker's compensation. Accidents traveling to work or unrelated illnesses are NOT covered.

49) Correct Answer: D

Explanation: All the examples depict reasonable accommodations for housing under the Fair Housing Act, which are required by law.

50) Correct Answer: C

Explanation: The standard commission split gives 60% to the listing brokerage and 40% to a selling/showing agent from another brokerage. On a 5% commission, this equates to 3% and 2%.

Multiple Choice Questions: State-Specific Section

Q1.   According to [state] landlord-tenant law, what is the maximum security deposit a landlord can charge for an unfurnished apartment?

    A.   One month's rent

    B.   Two month's rent

    C.   First and last month's rent

    D.   No limit is defined

Q2.   Under [state] law, which of the following real estate license applicants must complete a 40-hour pre-licensure course?

    A.   In-state applicants only

    B.   Out-of-state applicants only

    C.   All new license applicants

    D.   Licensees reinstating a license

Q3.   According to [state] transaction brokerage laws, which of the following actions by a transaction broker would violate agency duties?

    A.   Disclosing confidential client information

    B.   Recommending price reductions to both parties

    C.   Providing comparable market data to clients

    D.   Drafting a purchase offer for the buyer's signature

Q4.   Which of the following single-family residential properties would be exempt from [state's] mandatory radon disclosure requirements prior to sale?

    A.   A new construction home

    B.   An estate sale property

    C.   A foreclosure property

    D.   A home never tested for radon

Q5.   In [state], the agency responsible for regulating the sale of real estate securities and builder-developer licenses is the:

A.   Department of Real Estate

B.   Department of Corporations

C.   Department of Financial Protection

D.   Department of Transportation

Q6.   Under the commissions section of [state's] listing agreements, the seller has the right to:

A.   Set maximum commission rates

B.   Determine the brokerage split

C.   Cancel commissions if unsatisfied

D.   Receive an accounting of commissions

Q7.   According to [state] advertising laws, which of the following MUST be included in ads for mortgage loans?

A.   License number of lender

B.   Disclaimer of fees for quotes

C.   Notice of interpreter availability

D.   All of the above

Q8.   Under [state] agency disclosure law, a dual agent is REQUIRED to disclose:

A.   Property defects are known by the brokerage

B.   Confidential information about either party

C.   The buyer's financial qualification details

D.   That confidentiality duties still exist

Q9.   According to [state] laws, where must the seller's property condition disclosure form be posted when completed?

A.   Multiple Listing Service

B.   Company listing database

C.   Appraiser's files

D.   Shown to prospective buyers

Q10.   Under [state's] definition of agency relationships, which of the following requirements applies to ALL agents?

    A.   Loyalty to clients

    B.   Promotion of client's interests

    C.   Obedience to lawful client requests

    D.   Reasonable skill and care

Q11.   According to [state] license law, which of the following activities is permitted for unlicensed assistants under the supervision of a managing broker?

    A.   Hosting open houses

    B.   Preparing promotional materials

    C.   Explaining listing agreements

    D.   Soliciting sellers for listings

Q12.   Under [state] fair housing regulations, which of the following reasonable modifications must landlords permit for residents with disabilities?

    A.   Installing ramps at entrances

    B.   Adding lever-style handles on doors

    C.   Altering shower floors to eliminate barriers

    D.   All of the above

Q13.   A [state] brokerage firm's trust account receives a check for $30,000 as an earnest money deposit on one transaction. The brokerage balance PRIOR to the deposit was $5,000. If the brokerage writes a check the next day for an owner advance of $8,000, what is the new account balance?

    A. $27,000

    B. $29,000

    C. $32,000

    D. $37,000

Q14.   Under [state] core course education requirements, new salesperson licensees must complete at least the following:

A.   12 instructional hours

B.   18 instructional hours

C.   24 instructional hours

D.   45 instructional hours

Q15.   According to [state] law, which of the following types of compensation arrangements between brokers are prohibited?

A.   Profit-sharing

B.   Bonus commissions

C.   Referral fees

D.   Fee splitting

Q16.   Under [state's] home seller disclosure law, when must a seller provide the completed property disclosure form to buyers?

A.   At the initial showing

B.   After the offer is accepted

C.   Before the buyer's first visit for a showing

D.   During the inspection period

Q17.   Under [state's] licensing laws, how LONG can a brokerage firm display the license of a salesperson who has terminated their association?

A.   1 week

B.   2 weeks

C.   1 month

D.   6 months

Q18.   According to [state] landlord-tenant laws, what is the maximum late fee that can be charged for an overdue rental payment?

A. $15

B. $50

C.   5% of the monthly rent

D.   10% of the monthly rent

Q19.   A [state] seller fails to disclose a known roof defect at the time of sale. Under [state] law, when does the statute of limitations expire for the buyers to file a lawsuit against the seller?

A.   1 year from sale date

B.   18 months from the sale date

C.   2 years from sale date

D.   5 years from sale date

Q20.   Under [state] agency law, a seller's agent owes fiduciary duties to the:

A.   Buyer

B.   Seller

C.   Seller's family members

D.   Appraiser

Q21.   According to advertising regulations in [state], real estate ads MUST disclose the brokerage agency relationship if an agent's name or photo is used. If no agent is named or pictured, the ad must disclose:

A.   Brokerage's number of years in business

B.   Physical office address of brokerage

C.   Brokerage license number

D.   No disclosure is required

Q22.   Under [state] agency law, a buyer wishes to see a property owned by the broker's friend. The broker MUST:

A.   Assign an agent who knows the owner to show the property.

B.   Accompany their friend to personally point out property features.

C.   Act only as a transaction broker in dealings with the buyer.

D.   Disclose their relationship before any showing occurs.

Q23.   According to [state] licensing regulations, a real estate salesperson convicted of a felony within the past 5 years is:

A.   Permitted to apply if the conviction did not involve real estate

B.   Not eligible to apply for 10 years after conviction

C.   Eligible if the crime did not involve moral turpitude

D.   Never again eligible for licensure

Q24.   Under [state's] anti-discrimination law, which of the following is classified as a protected class in housing transactions?

A.   Smokers

B.   Veterans

C.   Recipients of housing assistance

D.   Parents with children under 18

Q25.   According to [state] advertising guidelines, promotional materials for a new condominium development sent by mail MUST include the following:

A.   Number of units already sold

B.   Developer's total years of experience

C.   Terms of availability for inspection

D.   Name of salesperson for the project

Q26.   Under [state's] broker supervision requirements, licensees may NOT perform which action without broker oversight?

A.   Host open houses

B.   Prepare listing presentations

C.   Draft offers and contracts

D.   Analyze market trends

Q27.   A [state] broker is sponsoring a new salesperson licensee. For the FIRST two years of licensure, the supervising broker must:

A.   Provide weekly progress reports on the licensee.

B.   Actively oversee all contracts prepared by the licensee.

C.   Continuously train and review the licensee's practices.

D.   Conduct bi-monthly reviews of the licensee's files.

Q28.   According to [state] agency disclosure requirements, a real estate licensee MUST reveal their agency relationship:

A.   At first contact with new clients

B.   Within 3 days of meeting new clients

C.   Before preparing a purchase offer

D.   Upon finalizing a representation agreement

Q29.   Under [state's] rules for real estate teams, which of the following activities is permitted by unlicensed team members?

    A.   Receiving referral fees from vendors

    B.   Providing property staging services for clients

    C.   Assisting with market research and analysis

    D.   Securing vendor services under the team's name

Q30.   According to advertising guidelines in [state], an attorney advertises discounted services for completing quick real estate closings. The ad MUST include the attorney's:

    A.   Bar disciplinary history

    B.   Malpractice insurance coverage

    C.   Fees for all standard services

    D.   License to practice law

Answer Key

1)   Correct Answer: B

Explanation: [State] law limits security deposits on unfurnished rentals to a maximum of 2 month's rent. Landlords can charge higher deposits for furnished units.

2)   Correct Answer: C

Explanation: [State] requires all NEW real estate license applicants, whether from in-state or out-of-state, to complete 40 hours of approved pre-licensure education. License reinstatement has different requirements.

3)   Correct Answer: A

Explanation: Disclosing confidential client information would violate [state] transaction brokerage agency. Providing market data, drafting offers, and making recommendations are permitted brokerage activities.

4)   Correct Answer: A

Explanation: Only newly constructed single-family homes that have never been occupied are exempt from [state's] radon disclosure laws for residential home sellers. Foreclosures, estate sales, and non-tested homes require disclosure.

5)   Correct Answer: B

Explanation: [State's] Department of Corporations oversees the permitting and regulation of real estate securities issuers and licenses for developers. Other agencies govern other aspects of real estate.

6)   Correct Answer: D

Explanation: [State] sellers have the right to receive an accounting of commissions and splits - BUT they cannot dictate rates/terms or arbitrarily cancel earned commissions.

7)   Correct Answer: D

Explanation: [State's] mortgage advertising laws require ads to include the license number of the lender, disclaimer of fees just for loan quotes, and notice of free interpreter services. All the answers are required.

8)   Correct Answer: D

Explanation: Dual agents in [state] are only REQUIRED to disclose that confidentiality duties still exist to both parties - they cannot disclose confidential information or finances.

9)   Correct Answer: D

Explanation: In [state], the property condition disclosure form must be completed by the seller and shown/provided to potential buyers - it does not get filed elsewhere.

10)   Correct Answer: D

Explanation: Reasonable skill/care is required of ALL agents under all agency relationships in [state]. Loyalty, promotion of interests, and obedience are required only under specific agency relationships.

11)   Correct Answer: B

Explanation: Unlicensed assistants in [state] may prepare promotional materials under supervision. They CANNOT solicit clients, host open houses, or explain contracts that require a license.

12)   Correct Answer: D

Explanation: [State] landlords must allow unit modifications like ramps, lever handles, and accessible showers as reasonable accommodations for residents with disabilities.

13)   Correct Answer: C

Explanation:

Beginning balance: $5,000 Deposit: + $30,000 Withdraw: - $8,000

New Balance: $5,000 + $30,000 - $8,000 = $32,000

14)   Correct Answer: C

Explanation: [State] requires new salesperson licensees to complete a 24+ hour core course within their first license renewal period covering key real estate concepts. Other answers provide too few minimum hours.

15)   Correct Answer: D

Explanation: [State's] anti-rebate law prohibits fee splitting between brokers to avoid rebating to attract clients. Profit-sharing, bonuses, and referrals are permitted.

16)   Correct Answer: C

Explanation: In [state], the seller disclosure must be provided to a buyer BEFORE the first visit to view the property to allow time to review before touring/making an offer.

17)   Correct Answer: B

Explanation: [State] allows brokerages to display terminated agents' licenses up to 2 weeks after termination while winding down business relationships. One week is too short, and a month or more is too long.

18)   Correct Answer: C

Explanation: [State] law limits late fees on overdue rent to 5% of the monthly rental amount. Flat fees over $50 and 10% would exceed the maximum allowed fee.

19)   Correct Answer: C

Explanation: In [state], buyers have up to 2 years from the sale date to file a legal action against the seller for nondisclosure of known defects. The other timeframes would occur too soon or late.

20)   Correct Answer: B

Explanation: Seller's agents owe fiduciary duties only to their client - the seller - not the buyer, seller's family, appraiser, etc. This reflects agency loyalty in [state].

21)   Correct Answer: C

Explanation: [State's] advertising rules require brokerage license number disclosure in ads without an agent name/photo. Years in business, office address, and no disclosure are incorrect.

22)   Correct Answer: D

Explanation: The broker must disclose their relationship with the seller BEFORE showing to avoid conflict of interest. They cannot act as the buyer's agent or transaction broker without notice.

23)   Correct Answer: B

Explanation: [State] prohibits applying for a real estate license for 10 years following a felony conviction. After 10 years, they may be eligible, depending on the crime.

24)   Correct Answer: C

Explanation: [State] law prohibits housing discrimination against recipients of housing vouchers and similar assistance. Veterans, smokers, and families are not protected classes.

25)   Correct Answer: C

Explanation: Condo mail promotions in [state] must disclose terms to inspect the property. Other answers are not mandatory.

26)   Correct Answer: C

Explanation: [State] requires brokers to supervise any preparation of legal contracts by licensees. Licensees CAN perform other promotional/sales functions independently.

27)   Correct Answer: C

Explanation: [State] supervising brokers must continuously train and actively review sponsored licensees for the first two years of practice. Formal reports are not required.

28)   Correct Answer: D

Explanation: [State] agents must disclose their agency relationship when finalizing the representation agreement with a new client before accessing confidential information.

29)   Correct Answer: C

Explanation: Unlicensed team members may assist with administrative tasks like market research/analysis in [state]. Referral fees, staging, and securing vendor services under the team's brand all require proper licensing.

30)   Correct Answer: D

Explanation: Attorney ads offering real estate services in [state] must indicate the attorney's license to prove qualification and authority. Other disclosures are not required.

Conclusion

As we reach the end of this journey into the intricate world of real estate, I hope you are feeling equipped with the knowledge required to excel on the upcoming licensing exam—and, equally importantly—to flourish in your new career.

While the industry has untold potential for enterprising professionals, the sheer breadth of laws, guidelines, and procedures can seem daunting at first. My aim with this book was to methodically break down key material, ensuring you have a foundational grasp not just for the exam but for navigating real-world real estate transactions with confidence.

We began by exploring theoretical pillars—the principles governing property ownership, land usage, market valuation, legal contracts, agency relationships, and financing procedures. These chapters solidified your understanding of real estate's underlying framework. Next, to account for state-by-state variability, I highlighted regulations specific to 10 prominent states while also arming you with strategies for identifying local rules in your specific exam jurisdiction.

Transitioning to hands-on exam prep, I shared practical techniques for efficient study habits and provided opportunities to apply knowledge through scenarios and quizzes. The math workbook enabled you to sharpen computational skills, while the final mock exam simulated the actual testing experience to gauge your readiness.

My sincere hope is that you now feel fully equipped and empowered to flourish in the real estate profession and align your passion with your purpose. I encourage you to embrace productive habits that will fuel an ongoing love of learning. Stay curious, continue reading industry materials, and never hesitate to ask mentors questions as you navigate new professional challenges.

While exams can feel intimidating, remember that tests merely capture a moment in time. What truly counts is the knowledge you will carry forth into your blossoming career. Let the content within these pages be guideposts as you embark on this exciting journey. I am confident you have what it takes to excel as a real estate salesperson. Believe in your potential, and the industry's endless opportunities for growth will open before you.

The day will soon arrive when you proudly hold your new license in hand. When you look back, view this book as just your first step into a lifelong, rewarding profession. Allow your passion for guiding clients and unearthing the perfect property match to fuel your success. But never rest on your laurels—keep building your skills and expanding your knowledge base. This industry rewards expertise, innovation, and service.

You have chosen a career field that allows you to harness ambition and channel your people skills towards profoundly impacting lives. There will be challenges ahead, but with dedication and the right mindset, you have all the tools needed to flourish. I wish you the very best as you embark on this exciting journey into the world of real estate. Believe in yourself, and take pride in helping guide others towards the dream of home ownership.

EXTRA CONTENT DOWNLOAD

This is my way of saying thank you
to my loyal readers!
SCAN THE QR-CODE BELOW
TO DOWNLOAD YOUR EXTRA CONTENT!

Should you encounter any issues downloading it, please write to:

info@abbotwardman.com – our team will send it to you.

As in any growth journey, your feedback is invaluable.

I invite you to share your opinion by leaving a review of this book on Amazon.com

SCAN THIS QRCODE

THANK YOU FOR YOUR SUPPORT, IT'S TRULY VALUABLE TO ME!

Made in the USA
Las Vegas, NV
26 September 2024